BASIC / NOT BORING MATH SKILLS

PRE-ALGEBRA

Grades 6–8+

Inventive Exercises to Sharpen
Skills and Raise Achievement

Series Concept & Development
by Imogene Forte & Marjorie Frank
Exercises by Marjorie Frank

Incentive Publications, Inc.
Nashville, Tennessee

About the cover:

Bound resist, or tie dye, is the most ancient known method of fabric surface design. The brilliance of the basic tie dye design on this cover reflects the possibilities that emerge from the mastery of basic skills.

Illustrated by Kathleen Bullock
Cover art by Mary Patricia Deprez, dba Tye Dye Mary®
Cover design by Marta Drayton, Joe Shibley, and W. Paul Nance
Edited by Angela L. Reiner

ISBN 978-0-86530-447-5

6   7   8   9   10   11   10   09   08

PRINTED IN THE UNITED STATES OF AMERICA
www.incentivepublications.com

TABLE OF CONTENTS

CELEBRATE BASIC
MATH SKILLS

Basic does not mean boring! There certainly is nothing dull about . . .

- . . . using integers to help daring hikers pack up for an adventure, blaze trails, scale mountains, or brave cold temperatures

- . . . using your math skills to keep pace with the elevator in the camping store

- . . . check out the weight of some tasty camping food

- . . . finding the right equation to escape a hungry bear

- . . . figuring out who takes the longest to set up the tent or who gathers the most firewood

- . . . calculating amounts of blisters, marshmallows, ghost stories, or weird noises in the night

- . . . getting algebra to help campers turn a backwards canoe around in the rapids

- . . . tracking down missing chocolate bars or finding a lost hiker

- . . . solving problems about daring rock climbs, poison ivy, or bothersome insects

These are just a few of the interesting adventures students can explore as they celebrate basic math skills with pre-algebra activities. The idea of celebrating the basics is just what it sounds like—sharpening math skills while enjoying the exciting escapades of some adventuresome campers. Each page of this book invites students to practice a high-interest math exercise about a group of friends who are off on a wilderness trip. This is not just any ordinary fill-in-the-blanks way to learn. These exercises are fun and surprising, and they make good use of thinking skills. Students will do the useful work of practicing specific pre-algebra skills while stepping into a world of daredevil activities and wild fun.

The pages in this book can be used in many ways . . .

- for individual students to sharpen a particular skill

- with a small group needing to relearn or sharpen a skill

- as an instructional tool for teaching a skill to any size group

- by students working on their own

- by students working under the direction of an adult.

Each page may be used to introduce a new skill, to reinforce a skill, or to assess a student's ability to perform a skill. You'll also find an appendix of resources helpful to students and teachers—including a ready-to-use test for assessing pre-algebra skills.

As your students take on the challenges of these adventures with pre-algebra, they will grow! And as you watch them check off the basic math skills they've strengthened, you can celebrate with them!

7

SKILLS CHECKLIST FOR PRE-ALGEBRA

✔	SKILL	PAGE(S)
	Identify opposites for positive and negative integers	10
	Give the absolute value of an integer	10
	Compare and order integers	11
	Add integers	12
	Subtract integers	13
	Multiply integers	14
	Divide integers	15
	Solve real-world problems with integers	16
	Describe relationships between numbers	17
	Evaluate mathematical expressions	18
	Write mathematical expressions	19
	Identify terms, variables, and coefficients in mathematical expressions	20
	Simplify mathematical expressions	21, 22
	Choose expressions to match statements	23
	Write expressions to match statements	24
	Choose equations to solve problems	25
	Write equations to solve problems	26
	Rewrite equations using inverse operations	27
	Identify and use number properties	28, 29
	Solve one-step equations with one variable	30, 31
	Solve multi-step equations with one variable	32, 33
	Determine accuracy of solutions	33, 35
	Solve equations with rational numbers	34
	Use equations to solve real-world problems	36, 37
	Solve inequalities	38, 39
	Graph inequalities	39
	Solve equations with two variables	40, 41, 44, 45
	Locate ordered pairs of numbers on a coordinate plane	42, 43
	Graph equations with two variables	44, 45
	Identify transformations	46, 47
	Identify corresponding points in transformations	46, 47
	Identify and extend patterns and sequences	48, 49
	Solve proportions	50

PRE-ALGEBRA

Skills Exercises

SHOWING OFF INTEGERS

A bunch of friends are making plans for a camping trip. Each of them is wearing a T-shirt with a different integer. Figure out the opposites and values of their integers.
Look at the T-shirt for each kid shown
on these two pages (10 and 11).

> The **absolute value** of an integer is its distance from zero on a number line. **Opposites** have the same absolute value.

Give this information for the integer on the shirt:

1. **Chad**
   a. Is it positive (P) or negative (N)? _____
   b. What is the absolute value? _____
   c. What is its opposite? _____

2. **Zoey**
   a. P or N ? _____
   b. absolute value _____
   c. opposite _____

3. **Mike**
   a. P or N ? _____
   b. absolute value _____
   c. opposite _____

4. **Sam**
   a. P or N ? _____
   b. absolute value _____
   c. opposite _____

5. **Yolanda**
   a. P or N ? _____
   b. absolute value _____
   c. opposite _____

6. **Matt**
   a. P or N ? _____
   b. absolute value _____
   c. opposite _____

7. **Basha**
   a. P or N ? _____
   b. absolute value _____
   c. opposite _____

8. **Toni**
   a. P or N ? _____
   b. absolute value _____
   c. opposite _____

Name _____

A MATTER OF ORDER

Don't be fooled by integers! Some of them look bigger or smaller than they really are.

Look at the integers on pages 10 and 11.
Answer these questions.

1. How many t-shirts have integers > Zoey's? _____

2. How many are > Chad's? _____

3. How any are < Basha's? _____

4. How many are > Toni's? _____

5. How many are < Yolanda's? _____

6. How many are < Toni's? _____

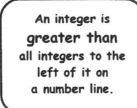

| An integer is **greater than** all integers to the left of it on a number line. | An integer is **less than** all integers to the right of it on a number line. |

Compare the two integers. Write > or < on each line.

7.	5 ____ 0		11.	0 ____ –3
8.	–2 ____ 2		12.	–8 ____ 6
9.	3 ____ –7		13.	0 ____ –7
10.	–4 ____ –8		14.	–6 ____ –11

15. Put the T-shirt integers in order from smallest to largest. _____

Write the integers in order from smallest to largest.

16. **20, –20, 4, –7, 3, 0, 6, –1** _____

17. **–8, –16, 3, –4, –3, 5, 10** _____

18. **2, –2, 6, 8, –8, –4, 4** _____

19. **0, 2, 6, 8, 7, –7, –12** _____

20. **11, 0, 5, –6, 2, 9, –8** _____

Name _____

MOUNTAIN UPS & DOWNS

The easiest trail to the top of Mt. Blister is eight miles long. Toni and Chad are planning their trip up the mountain.

Last year, they covered 4 miles on Day #1 and 3 miles on Day #2. On Day #3, they went back down the trail 2 miles to recover from altitude sickness. On Day #4, they hiked up the mountain 1½ more miles Where were they at the end of Day #4?

This problem will show their forward and backward movements.

4 + 3 + –2 + 1½ = (mile) 6½

> The sum of 2 positive integers is **positive.**
> The sum of 2 negative integers is **negative.**
> The sum of a positive integer and a negative integer
> may be **positive, negative, or zero.**

Solve these addition problems.

1. 7 + –3 = _____

2. –6 + –9 = _____

3. –63 + –36 = _____

4. –8 + 12 = _____

5. 5 + –9 = _____

6. 7 + –6= _____

7. –10 + 10 = _____

8. –41 + –34 = _____

9. –7 + –12 _____

10. –2 + –3 = _____

11. –12 + –11 + –6 = _____

12. 6 + –3 + –11 + 9 + 5 = _____

13. 10 + –2 + –30 = _____

14. 6 + 2 + 9 + –25 = _____

15. –4 + 3 + 4 + –3 + 3 = _____

16. –50 + –12 + 3 = _____

17. 27 + 18 + –3 = _____

18. –27 + –1 + 7 = _____

Name _____

MOUNTAINOUS LOCATIONS

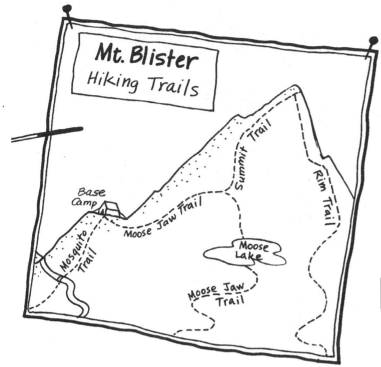

Mt. Blister
Hiking Trails

The hikers decide on the location for their Base Camp. They'll start their climb at 2 miles below Base Camp. By the end of the third day, they plan to be 4 miles above Base Camp. What is the difference between this goal and their starting location?

This problem will help to find the difference.

$4 - -2 =$ _____

> **To subtract an integer, add its opposite.**

Finish these.

1. $8 - 10 = 8 +$ _____

2. $8 - -10 = 8 +$ _____

3. $-8 - 10 = -8 +$ _____

4. $-8 - -10 = -8 +$ _____

5. $5 - 7 = 5 +$ _____

6. $5 - -7 = 5 +$ _____

7. $-5 - 7 = -5 +$ _____

8. $-5 - -7 = -5 +$ _____

Subtract these.

9. $2 - 2 =$ _____

10. $-8 - -4 =$ _____

11. $20 - -3 =$ _____

12. $-6 - 0 =$ _____

13. $-5 - -8 =$ _____

14. $12 - 22 =$ _____

15. $44 - -20 =$ _____

16. $-20 - -9 =$ _____

17. $14 - -5 =$ _____

18. $0 - -4 =$ _____

19. $0 - 4 =$ _____

20. $-33 - -4 =$ _____

21. Hot Springs is 4.3 miles up the trail from Base Camp. Juniper Hollow is 1.5 miles below Base Camp. What is the difference between the locations?

_____

Name _____

CHANGING BY DEGREES

Packing the right clothing for a camping trip is challenging, especially when mountains are a part of the trip plan. The temperatures on mountains are tricky, changing quickly with altitude or unexpected weather. The campers hear that there is a 5° temperature change for each thousand feet of altitude on Mt. Grizzly. The higher they go . . . the colder it gets!

I'll need a bathing suit and long johns!

Yolanda

If the temperature is 60° at 2000 feet elevation, what is the temperature at the base?

This formula will help you find out.
(t = temperature; b = base temperature;
n = thousands of feet)
$t = b + (n \times 5 \text{ or } -5)$
$t = 60 + (2 \times 5)$

If the temperature is 40° at the base, what is it at the 9000-foot peak?
$t = 40 + (9 \times -5)$

Finish the chart to compare temperatures on Mt. Grizzly.

The product of 2 positive integers is **positive**.
The product of 2 negative integers is **positive**.
The product of a positive integer and a negative integer is **negative**.

Expected Temperatures on Mt. Grizzly

	Temp at Base	1 thousand feet above base	2 thousand feet above base	4 thousand feet above base	6 thousand feet above base	9 thousand feet above base
1	30° F	25°	20°		0°	
2	42° F					
3	60° F					
4	16° F					
5	11° F					
6					- 20° F	

Multiply the integers.

7. $7 \times -10 =$ _____

8. $14 \times -3 =$ _____

9. $-10 \times -6 =$ _____

10. $7 \times -9 =$ _____

11. $-100 \times -100 =$ _____

Estimate the products.

12. $5 \times -498 =$ _____

13. $-102 \times -15 =$ _____

14. $-202 \times 1011 =$ _____

15. $78 \times -4 =$ _____

16. $-92 \times -7 =$ _____

Name _____

COLD CALCULATIONS

Even in the summer, it gets awfully cold on Mt. Grizzly. Campers need to make plans for chilly nights. As they are planning their trip, the campers pay close attention to the past records of daytime and nighttime temperatures on the mountain.

The quotient of 2 positive or 2 negative integers is **positive**.
The quotient of a positive and a negative integer is **negative**.

Mount Grizzly Peak
Average Nighttime Temperatures

Month	Daytime *Farenheit Temp*	Nighttime *Farenheit Temp*
Jan	-18°	-45°
Feb	-16°	-32°
Mar	-6°	-14°
Apr	5°	-7°
May	18°	10°
Jun	24°	12°
Jul	50°	20°
Aug	48°	-1°
Sept	36°	-8°
Oct	-5°	-15°
Nov	-2°	-20°
Dec	-28°	-35°

Divide integers to find the month that fits the description.

1. Night temperature is half as cold as Dec. daytime. _____

2. Night temperature is one-fifth as cold as Dec. nighttime._____

3. Day temperature is one-third as cold as Mar. daytime. _____

4. Day temperature is one-fourth as cold as Nov. nighttime._____

5. Night temperature is one-seventh as cold as Apr. nighttime. _____

6. Its daytime temperature is one-tenth as cold as its nighttime._____

7. Its daytime temperature is half as cold as its nighttime._____

8. Night temperature is one-third as cold as Jan. nighttime. _____

Divide the integers.

9. $100 \div -10 =$ _____

10. $-78 \div -6 =$ _____

11. $-1000 \div 10 =$ _____

12. $-80 \div -4 =$ _____

13. $-44 \div 11 =$ _____

14. $4000 \div -40 =$ _____

Name _____

ELEVATOR PUZZLERS

A visit to the Super Camp Store is on the schedule for today. Sam and Basha will ride the elevator to the right floors for their supplies. Pay attention to the labels by the buttons, and use integers to solve these elevator problems.

Write and solve an integer problem for each question.

1. They leave the camera floor, ride up two floors, and down three. What floor are they on?

_____

2. They leave the shoe & boot department and ride up ten floors. What floor are they on?

_____

3. What is on the floor that is twice the distance from ground floor as the camera floor?

_____

4. They leave the repair shop, ride up eight floors, and down one. What kind of merchandise will they find here?

_____

5. To go from the tent department to the repair shop, how many floors must they travel?

_____

6. What merchandise is on the floor that is 9 floors above the floor with kids' supplies?

_____

ELEVATOR

↑	8	CLIMBING GEAR
↑	7	VIDEOS, SLIDES
↑	6	BOOKS, MAPS
↑	5	COOKING UTENSILS
↑	4	CAMPING FOOD
↑	3	CLOTHING
↑	2	TENTS
↑	1	BACKPACKS
GROUND LEVEL		SLEEPING BAGS
↓	1	KID'S SUPPLIES
↓	2	CAMERAS
↓	3	SHOES, BOOTS
↓	4	REPAIR SHOP

7. What is on the floor that is one below the floor that is four floors above shoes & boots?

_____

8. They leave the clothing floor, ride down 3 floors, up 8 floors, and down two. What kind of merchandise will they find here?

_____

Name _____

WHO'S RELATED?

Some of the hikers are related to each other. Figure out these relationships while you explore the relationships between the numbers that describe their sizes and weights. The weights of the campers include the weight of the full pack.

MATT
Age: 8
Weight: 80 lb
Boot Size: 2

CHAD
Age: 15
Weight: 180 lb
Boot Size: 12

MIKE
Age: 18
Weight: 200 lb
Boot Size: 10

BASHA
Age: 16
Weight: 130 lb
Boot Size: 7

TONI
Age: 12
Weight: 120 lb
Boot Size: 6

1. Basha is 8 years less than twice the age of her cousin.
   Who is her cousin?_____

2. With pack, Matt weighs 20 pounds less than half as much as his brother.
   Who is his brother? _____

3. Chad's boot size is two less than twice his sister's.
   Who is his sister? _____

Which of these is true? Write T in front of the accurate relationships.

_____ 4. Basha's weight is greater than two other campers' weights.

_____ 5. Chad's age is 3 years less than twice Matt's.

_____ 6. Mike's boot size is half his age.

_____ 7. Mike's weight is equal to Matt's and Toni's combined.

Write a phrase that describes a way these two numbers are related.

8. Matt and Basha's ages: _____

9. Mike's and Toni's ages: _____

10. Chad's age and boot size: _____

11. Toni and Chad's weights: _____

12. Matt and Mike's boot sizes: _____

Name

TRUE EXPRESSIONS

$4w < c + b$!

This sentence makes sense to the shoppers.
Just look at the list of camping goods, and it will make sense to you, too.

It's an expression that uses numbers instead of words to tell you something.

In this case, it tells you that
the price of four water bottles is less than
the cost of a cook stove plus a pair of boots.

Is the above expression true? _____
You can tell by using the sale poster to find the money value of each letter (variable) in the expression.

Circle the expression that is true.

$t < 2s$ $\qquad$ $s > 2t$ $\qquad$ $2s = t$

SALE!!!
CAMPING SUPPLIES

t	tents	$ 200
s	sleeping bags	$ 180
b	boots	$ 160
p	packs	$ 240
c	cook stoves	$ 32
f	frying pans	$ 18
w	water bottles	$ 6

Find the mathematical expression to match each group of words below.

1. cost of three water bottles and two packs
   $3w + 2p$ $\qquad$ $3(w + p)$ $\qquad$ $3w \times 2p$

2. cost of four frying pans and one sleeping bag
   $4(f + s)$ $\qquad$ $4f + 4s$ $\qquad$ $4f + s$

3. ten dollars more than two cook stoves
   $c + 2s + 10$ $\qquad$ $10 - 2c$ $\qquad$ $2c + 10$

4. cost of a pair of boots less three dollars
   $3b + 3$ $\qquad$ $3b$ $\qquad$ $b - 3$ $\qquad$ $b + 3$

5. cost of a frying pan is less than two tents
   $f > t$ $\qquad$ $2f < 2t$ $\qquad$ $2f < 2t$ $\qquad$ $f < 2t$

6. three times the cost of a pack and boots
   $3p + b$ $\qquad$ $3(p + b)$ $\qquad$ $3p \times 3b$

7. two dollars more than five water bottles
   $(5-2)w$ $\qquad$ $5w + b$ $\qquad$ $5w + 2$

8. the cost of a cook stove, two water bottles, and a frying pan is less than one hundred dollars
   $c + 2w + f < 100$ $\qquad$ $100 - 2(c + w + f)$

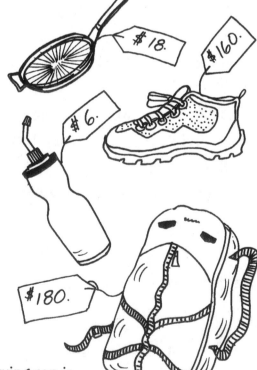

Name

EXPRESSIONS WITH TASTE

No hiker wants a back-breaking pack, so it's important to pay attention to weight while the supplies are gathered for the pack. These food items have weights (in ounces) that are represented by letter symbols.

For instance:
the weight of five boxes of raisins increased by the weight of eight chocolate bars is written.....
5r + 8c

These chocolate bars weigh a lot!
I better get rid of them all!

Hmmm!

Zoey

CAMPING FOOD

weight in ounces	food
m	maple oatmeal
n	noodle packs
s	cans of stew
a	apples
h	hot chocolate packs
r	boxes of raisins
c	chocolate bars
g	bags of gorp
f	fruit leather sticks
b	bread rolls
j	jerky sticks
p	power bars

Use the letter symbols to write mathematical expressions about the food weights.

Write an expression to show the weight of . . .

1. 1 bag of oatmeal increased by 3 ounces: _____

2. 15 boxes of raisins decreased by 7 jerky sticks: _____

3. 4 power bars decreased by 2 packs of noodles: _____

4. 12 bags of gorp decreased by 4 bags of gorp: _____

5. 8 chocolate bars decreased by 5 ounces: _____

6. twice the sum of 2 bread rolls and 6 jerky sticks: _____

7. 3 times the difference between 2 stew cans and 5 fruit leather sticks: _____

8. 10 hot chocolate packets increased by 1 stew can and 2 power bars: _____

9. 2 apples weigh less than 3 power bars: _____

10. 5 times the weight of a bread roll and an apple: _____

11. the sum of ½ bag of raisins and ¼ bag of gorp: _____

12. ten times the product of bread and fruit leather: _____

Name _____

ALGEBRA ON THE TRAIL

Study the route the hikers plan to take to Mt. Grizzly. On the first day, they plan to hike from Bear Paw Pond to Lake Achoo. The second day, they'll go on to Horsefly Pond. On Day 3, their trip will be four times the length of their first day. The last day will take them to the summit. They'll hike half as far as the first day.

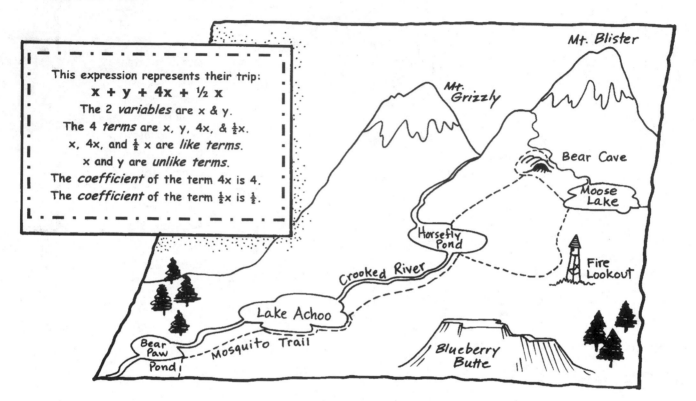

This expression represents their trip:

x + y + 4x + ½ x

The 2 *variables* are x & y.

The 4 *terms* are x, y, 4x, & ½x.

x, 4x, and ½ x are *like terms*.

x and y are *unlike terms*.

The *coefficient* of the term 4x is 4.

The *coefficient* of the term ½x is ½.

How many variables in each expression?

1. $2z - 9x$ _____

2. $-4b + 2a + -7a$ _____

3. $-9k + 2m$ _____

4. $p + q + 2(r - s)$ _____

Are the terms like(L) or unlike(U)?

5. $6x + 17x - 2x$ _____

6. $14y + 6x - x$ _____

7. $-3a + 2(c + b)$ _____

8. $-20 p + 6q$ _____

How many terms in each expression?

9. $y + \frac{1}{3}y$ _____

10. $-10p + 2\frac{1}{2}q + r - s$ _____

11. $2x + 3y + 9.9z > w$ _____

12. $3.5p$ _____

13. $a + 2b - 3c + 4d + f$ _____

14. **$7z + 18m \div \frac{1}{2}b$**

What are the terms in this expression?

_____

What is the coefficient of z? _____

What is the coefficient of m? _____

What is the coefficient of b? _____

Name

_____

SIMPLY FOLLOW THE TRAIL

Today's trip takes the energetic hikers a long way through the Mt. Blister Wilderness Area. They follow Mosquito Trail from Bear Paw Pond to Lake Achoo, then on to Horsefly Pond, the Fire Lookout, and Moose Lake. The day's final destination is Bear Cave.

This expression represents the distance of the day's hike:

$x + y + 2x + +x + z$

The expression can be simplified by combining like terms.

$3+x + y + z$

Simplify the following expressions.

1. $3a + 5a$ _____

2. $x + x$ _____

3. $14k - 6k$ _____

4. $18 c + c + \frac{1}{4}c$ _____

5. $y - 5 + 10y$ _____

6. $\frac{1}{2}x - \frac{1}{4}x + 2$ _____

7. $10t + 14 - 3t$ _____

8. $5.2k - 2k + 5$ _____

9. $4z + 5x - 3z + x$ _____

10. $2n + n + 4p$ _____

11. $y + x + y + x$ _____

12. $7g - 3s + 20g$ _____

13. $4m + 7m + 100$ _____

14. $4(w + 3) - 2w$ _____

15. $b + 2(b + 5)$ _____

16. $3(a + 2) + 4a$ _____

17. $n + 5(2 + 3n)$ _____

18. $6(x + y) - 3y$ _____

19. $12p \div 2 + 3p$ _____

20. $5s - 2(s + t)$ _____

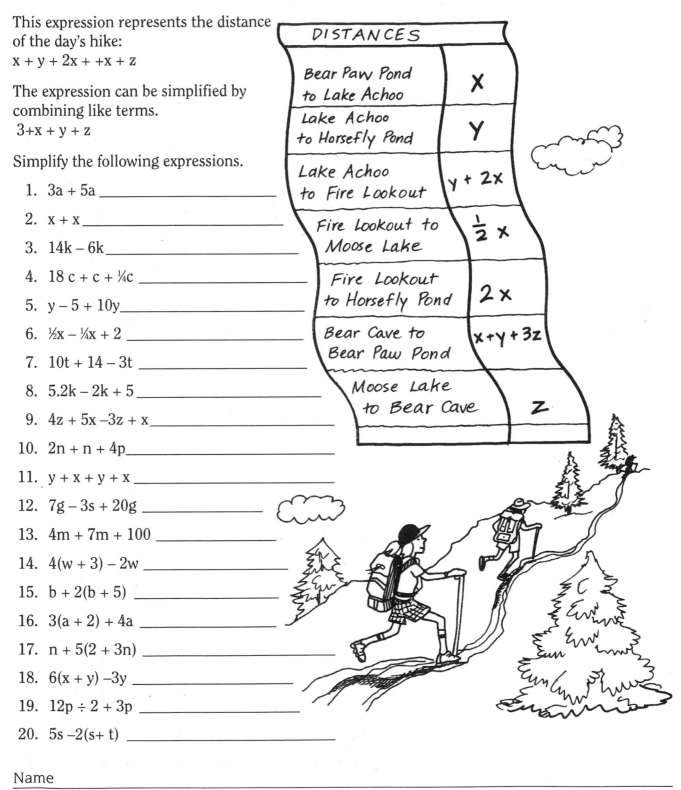

DISTANCES	
Bear Paw Pond to Lake Achoo	X
Lake Achoo to Horsefly Pond	Y
Lake Achoo to Fire Lookout	y + 2x
Fire Lookout to Moose Lake	$\frac{1}{2}$ x
Fire Lookout to Horsefly Pond	2 x
Bear Cave to Bear Paw Pond	x + y + 3z
Moose Lake to Bear Cave	z

Name _____

A SIMPLE TASK?

Setting up a tent ought to be simple for an experienced camper—right?
That's not quite the story for Chad. He's having some tent trouble today!
It took him a long, long time to get it right. It took Basha 25 minutes less. Toni set hers up in 38 minutes less than Chad, and Zoey took 30 minutes less. Matt beat them all by setting up his tent in 41 minutes less than Chad.

This expression shows how much time was spent setting up tents today, with Chad's time represented by **t**.

$t + (t-25) + (t-38) + (t-30) + (t-41)$

Here's the same expression simplified.

$5t - 134$

Simplify these equations by combining like terms.

1. $y + -3y + 10y + 7$

   _____

2. $5(x + 7) + -x$

   _____

3. $-p + 2p - -7p$

   _____

4. $\dfrac{-x + 3x + x}{5}$

   _____

5. $5z - 2z + 12$

   _____

6. $-t + 7t + 3t + 300$

   _____

7. $2(100y + 3) + y$

   _____

8. $12b + -8b + + b$

   _____

9. $45 + 6(a + b) + a$

   _____

10. $4(g + 6) - 6g$

    _____

11. $b + -d - -c + 3d$

    _____

12. $8x - 14x + 12$

    _____

13. $50 + 13p - 5 + 10p$

    _____

14. $4.5z - x - 7.5z$

    _____

15. $100j - -j + x - 2j$

    _____

16. $6(j + k) - 2j$

    _____

Name _____

22

EQUATIONS TO BOOT

At the end of a long hiking day, the boots are quickly pulled off the hot, aching feet. Use the boot statistics to practice your skills with equations.

Sam's boots are 3 sizes less than twice the size of Toni's. One of these equations represents his boot size.
(**s** = Sam's boot size; **t** = Toni's size)

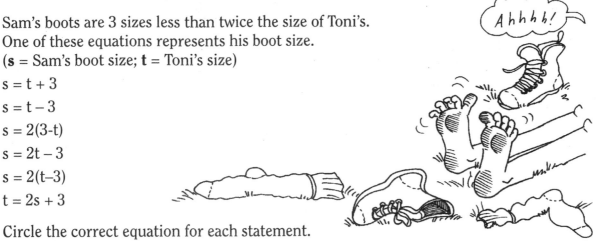

$s = t + 3$

$s = t - 3$

$s = 2(3-t)$

$s = 2t - 3$

$s = 2(t-3)$

$t = 2s + 3$

Circle the correct equation for each statement.

1. Basha's boots cost
   $80 more than Chad's.
   a. $b + 80 > c$
   b. $c = b + 80$
   c. $c + 80 = b$

2. Yolanda's boots cost $5 less than twice the cost of Sam's.
   a. $2s - 5 = y$
   b. $y + 5 = 2s$
   c. $5 + s = y$

3. Zoey's new boots cost $8 more than Toni's and Chad's combined.
   a. $z = t + c + 8$
   b. $2(t + c) = z - 8$
   c. $z + 8 = c + t$

4. Toni dried out her boots 4 hours more on Friday than on Thursday.
   a. $f + t = 4$
   b. $4f = t$
   c. $t + 4 = f$

5. On Monday, Mike's boots traveled 3 times longer than on Tuesday.
   a. $m \times t = 3$
   b. $t = 3m$
   c. $m = 3t$

6. On Sunday, Chad's boots traveled 6 miles less than on Wednesday.
   a. $w + 6 = s$
   b. $s + w = 6$
   c. $w - 6 = s$

7. Yolanda's boot size is one less than half the size of Chad's.
   a. $c = y - 1\frac{1}{2}$
   b. $y + \frac{1}{2} + 1 = c$
   c. $y = \frac{1}{2}c - 1$

8. Sam has 8 more than 4 times as many blisters on his left foot as on his right.
   a. $L = 8R + 4$
   b. $4R + 8 = L$
   c. $L + R = 4 \times 8$

9. Matt's right socks has 2 less than 6 times the holes as his left sock.
   a. $6L - 2 = R$
   b. $2(L + 6) = R$
   c. $R = (6 \times 2)$

10. Sam's socks have one more than twice the number of holes as Zoey's.
    a. $s = 2(z + 1)$
    b. $2z + 1 = s$
    c. $z = s + 1 \times 2$

Name

TO BUILD A FIRE

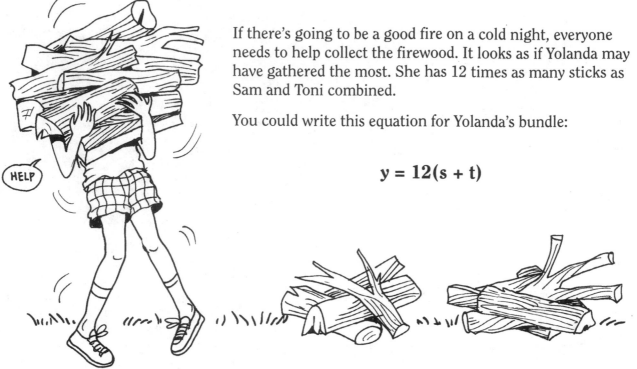

If there's going to be a good fire on a cold night, everyone needs to help collect the firewood. It looks as if Yolanda may have gathered the most. She has 12 times as many sticks as Sam and Toni combined.

You could write this equation for Yolanda's bundle:

$$y = 12(s + t)$$

Write an equation for each of these descriptions of the firewood situation.

1. Zoey *(z)* collected 3 more than twice Chad's (c) amount. _____

2. Toni gathered 5 less sticks than Matt and Basha did together. _____

3. Sam's bundle weighed 4 times Zoey's and Toni's together. _____

4. Yolanda searched for wood 5 less times than Sam did. _____

5. Toni carried 16 pounds less than Mike and Zoey together. _____

6. On Sunday, they burned 23 more pieces than on Thursday. _____

7. Basha collected 18 sticks more than Zoey collected. _____

8. On Saturday, they burned wood for 3 fewer hours than on Friday._____

9. The fire burned for one-fourth as long on Monday as on Tuesday. _____

10. On Monday, they burned 3 logs less than twice the amount burned on Saturday._____

11. The amount of wood burned on Monday and Wednesday totaled the same as the wood burned on Saturday and Tuesday._____

12. The temperature by the fire *(t)* was 5° less than three times the temperature away from the fire *(a)*. _____

Name

MARSHMALLOW PROBLEMS

The best part of the day is sitting around the campfire toasting those creamy, gooey marshmallows. Tonight is no exception, but there are a few problems with the marshmallows. For each marshmallow problem, choose the equation that would find a solution.

1. Critters ate 73 marshmallows total from 4 bags. 23 were eaten from Sam's bag, 6 from Chad's bag, and 18 from Matt's bag. How many were eaten from Mike's bag?
   a. $73 - 4 - 23 - 6 - 18 = x$
   b. $x = 23 + 6 + 18$
   c. $23 + 6 + 18 + x = 73$

Answer: _____

2. Basha dropped 2 marshmallows into the fire. Mike dropped 4 and Toni dropped 3. Yolanda dropped 4 times as many marshmallows into the fire as the other three campers combined. Mike, Basha, and Toni combined. How many did she drop?
   a. $x = 2 + 4 + 3 + 4$
   b. $x = 4(2 + 4 + 3)$
   c. $2 \times 4 \times 3 = x$

Answer: _____

3. In the last three nights, 24 marshmallows have been burned. On Tues., 4 more burned than on Mon. On Wed., 3 times as many were burned as on Mon. How many burned on Mon.?
   a. $24 - 4 - 3 = m$
   b. $m + (m + 4) + 3m = 24$
   c. $24 = 4(3 + 4)$

Answer: _____

4. Someone (or something) ate ½ bag of marshmallows. 1¾ bags were left. How many bags of marshmallows were there to begin?
   a. $1\frac{3}{4} + \frac{1}{2} = x$
   b. $x = 1\frac{3}{4} - \frac{1}{2}$
   c. $1\frac{3}{4} + x = \frac{1}{2}$

Answer: _____

5. Zoey ate 6 marshmallows on Tues. and 3 less on Wed. and 4 times as many on Mon. as on Tues. How many did she eat?
   a. $m = 6 + 3 + 4$
   b. $m = 6 + (6 - 3) + (4 \times 6)$
   c. $4(6 - 3) + 6 = m$

Answer: _____

6. Three campers ate 50 marshmallows one night. Toni ate 6. Chad ate 4 times as many as Toni and Sam combined. How many did Sam eat?
   a. $50 - 6 - 4n$
   b. $50 = 6 + n + 4(n + 6)$
   c. $6 + 4(n + 6) = 50$

Answer: _____

7. The group cooked 18 marshmallows. Sam ate 2 less than ½ of these. How many did he eat?
   a. $n = 18 \div 2 - 2$
   b. $18 - 2 + \frac{1}{2} = n$
   c. $n = 18 \times 2 - 2$

Answer: _____

Name _____

CANOE CALCULATIONS

The whole time Toni is trudging across the path carrying her canoe, she's calculating how much further she has left to walk. Sometimes she even counts steps or seconds. It always seems endless!

Help her with some canoe calculations. Write an equation that will solve each of the problems. Then find the solutions.

1. Toni has carried the canoe for 14 minutes. The trip should take 21 minutes. How much more time *(t)* does she have to walk?

    Equation: _____

    Answer: _____

2. The canoe weighs thirty pounds less than Toni. She weighs 100 pounds. What is the canoe's weight *(w)*?

    Equation: _____

    Answer: _____

3. The trail is 280 feet long. She has walked 20 feet less than half of this distance. How far *(d)* has she walked?

    Equation: _____

    Answer: _____

4. Matt has rested 3 times. Zoey has rested 6 times. Toni has rested twice as many times as Matt and Zoey combined. How many times has she rested *(r)*?

    Equation: _____

    Answer: _____

5. Chad carried Mike's canoe for 25 minutes. The trip took 50 minutes. How many minutes did Mike *(m)* carry his own canoe?

    Equation: _____

    Answer: _____

6. Toni dropped her canoe 9 times. This was 3 times less than twice the number of times Basha did. How many times did Basha drop her canoe *(d)*?

    Equation: _____

    Answer: _____

7. The canoe weighs 70 pounds. Toni weighs 100 pounds. With her pack and canoe, she weighs 208 pounds. How much does the pack weigh *(p)*?

    Equation: _____

    Answer: _____

Name _____

Basic Skills/Pre-Algebra 6-8+

REVERSE TRAVELS

The words reverse, inverse, opposite, or backwards could all be used to describe Sam's canoe trip through the rapids today. Whichever word you choose, he's still pointed in the wrong direction!

Inverse is a word that will help you solve equations. To find a solution, you will often need to get rid of the terms on the side of the equation with the variable. You do this by using inverse operations.

Add, subtract, multiply, or divide both sides of an equation by the same number to get an equivalent equation that will help you solve the problem. Use an inverse operation to rewrite and solve each equation caught in the rapids.

The examples will help you review this process.

1. $x + 8 = 20$
   $x + 8 - \underline{} = 20 - \underline{}$
   $x = \underline{}$

2. $p - 40 = -300$
   $p - 40 + \underline{} = -300 + \underline{}$
   $p = \underline{}$

3. $5c = -35$
   $5c/5 = -35/\underline{}$
   $c = \underline{}$

4. $y/6 = -8$
   $y/6 \times \underline{} = -8 \times \underline{}$
   $y = \underline{}$

5. $x + 15 = 7$

6. $q - 25 = -15$

7. $7r = -84$

8. $z/7 = -8$

Name

WHERE'S THE WATER?

On a hot, dusty trail, the climbers take out their water bottles. They have 7 water bottles. Each one has 0 ounces of water left in it. When they calculate how much water they have, they come up with ZERO. That's because 7 times 0 is ZERO. (It's also because they forgot to fill those bottles.)

The zero property for multiplication describes what happened to the thirsty climbers. The product of any number and zero is zero.

Here are examples of several number properties that are used when solving equations.

Which property is used?
Write the property for each equation.

Examples of Number Properties	
Identity Properties	$a + 0 = a$ and $a \times 1 = a$
Zero Property	$a \times 0 = 0$
Commutative Properties	$a + b = b + a$
	and $a \times b = b \times a$
Distributive Property	$a \times (b + c) = a \times b + a \times c$
Associative Properties	$(a + b) + c = a + (b + c)$
	and $(a \times b) \times c = a \times (b \times c)$
Opposites Properties	Dividing a number is the opposite of multiplying by that number. Subtracting a number is the opposite of adding that number.

I'm so dry!

Basha

1. $-40 \times 1 = -40$ _____

2. $-8 + (6 + -6) = -8$ _____

3. $-2 + (12 + 9) = (-2 + 12) + 9$ _____

4. $-9 \times 3 = 3 \times -9$ _____

5. $4 \times (-2 + 10) = (4 \times -2) + (4 \times 10)$ _____

6. $4 \times (-3 \times 2) = (4 \times -3) + (4 \times 2)$ _____

7. $7 \times -8 = -8 \times 7$ _____

8. $-200 + 0 = -200$ _____

9. $-200 \times 0 = 0$ _____

10. $-10 \times 1 = -10$ _____

11. $-9 + 4 = -5$ is the same as $-5 - 4 = -9$ _____

12. $(-20 + 5) + -3 = -20 + (5 + -3)$ _____

13. $3 \times -6 = -18$ is the same as $-18 \div -6$ _____

14. $14.5 + -99 = -99 + 14.5$ _____

15. $1 \times 16.5 = 16.5$ _____

16. $0 \times 1/2 = 0$ _____

Name _____

WHERE'S THE CHOCOLATE?

Basha is trying to figure out what has happened to all her chocolate bars. Her list tells how many she's borrowed, eaten, melted, or given away. However, she is not sure how many she has lost from friends. She uses the opposites property to help her solve the problem.

Use number properties to figure out which solution is correct for each equation.

Circle the correct solution.

1. $-3 \times 4 = n \times -3$
   a. $n = 3$
   b. $n = -3$
   c. $n = 4$
   d. $n = -4$

2. $22 + -12 = y + 22$
   a. $y = 12$
   b. $y = -12$
   c. $y = -22$
   d. $y = 0$

3. $8 + (q + 3) = 0$
   a. $q = 11$
   b. $q = 5$
   c. $q = -5$
   d. $q = -11$

commutative   distributive

identity   associative

zero property   opposites

CHOCOLATE BARS
Started with   15
Gave away   4
Melted   2
Borrowed   5
Lost   ?
Ate   9
Left over   2
How many lost?
$15 - 4 - 2 + 5 - X - 9 = 2$
$5 - X = 2$
$5 - X - 5 = 2 - 5$
$-X = -3$
$X = 3$

4. $15 \times d = 15$
   a. $d = 15$
   b. $d = 0$
   c. $d = 1$
   d. $d = -15$

5. $-6 + 3 = 3 + s$
   a. $s = 3$
   b. $s = -6$
   c. $s = 6$
   d. $s = 9$

6. $6 \times (3 + -9) =$
   $6 \times 3 + g \times -9$
   a. $g = 6$
   b. $g = -6$
   c. $g = 12$
   d. $g = 18$

7. $-20 + t = -20$
   a. $t = 20$
   b. $t = 1$
   c. $t = 0$
   d. $t = -20$

8. $1000 + (600 + 300) =$
   $(1000 + k) + 300$
   a. $k = 900$
   b. $k = 300$
   c. $k = 1900$
   d. $k = 600$

9. $25 \times 6 = j \times 25$
   a. $j = 25$
   b. $j = -6$
   c. $j = 6$
   d. $j = -25$

10. $-900 p = 0$
    a. $p = 900$
    b. $p = -1$
    c. $p = 100$
    d. $p = 0$

11. $4 \times (-4 \times 5) = -16 + b$
    a. $b = 4$
    b. $b = 5$
    c. $b = 20$
    d. $b = -4$

12. $-50 \times c = -50$
    a. $c = -1$
    b. $c = 1$
    c. $c = 0$
    d. $c - -50$

Name _____

WITH LIGHTNING ACCURACY

The storm has been raging for hours, and the campers have counted 150 lightning strikes in the last hour alone. To find out how many times lightning has struck per minute on the average, they've used the equation 60t = 150. Their solution is 2.5 times per minute.
Is this correct? _____

Examine their other solutions. If a solution is correct, circle the problem number. If it is not correct, cross out their solution and write the correct one.

1. $12x = 72$ $x = 6$ _____

2. $n \div 25 = 6$ $n = 150$ _____

3. $4 - -p = 27$ $p = 23$ _____

4. $1250 = \frac{1}{4} q$ $q = 250$ _____

5. $-10k = 360$ $k = 36$ _____

6. $d - 10.3 = 8.1$ $d = 18.4$ _____

7. $-100 = b + 6$ $b = 94$ _____

8. $-8x = -168$ $x = 21$ _____

9. $189 = 21r$ $r = 9$ _____

10. $\frac{m}{9} = 30$ $m = 270$ _____

11. $333 = \frac{1}{3} t$ $t = 999$ _____

12. $5\frac{1}{2} v = 99$ $v = 18$ _____

13. $\frac{n}{12} = -5$ $n = 60$ _____

14. $-7 - g = -49$ $g = 42$ _____

15. $x^2 = 64$ $x = 8$ _____

16. $\frac{s}{-100} = -10$ $s = -1000$ _____

17. $-11g = 22$ $g = -22$ _____

18. $400 = 50y$ $y = 8$ _____

Name

PUDDLE PUZZLER

It has rained for 7 hours. The puddles are gathering in all the tents. If 1.75 inches of rain have fallen in that time, how many inches fell per hour?_____
The equation $1.75 = 7x$ will help you find the amount.

Solve the equations below to complete the puddle

Across		Down	
A. $x + 100 = 146$	T. $2t = 98$	B. $1000 - g = 400$	Q. $2p = 1036$
E. $\frac{x}{3} = 9$	U. $g + 92 = 400$	C. $\frac{x}{3} = 9$	T. $\frac{1}{4} t = 1029$
G. $2200 - g = 89$	V. $120 = x - -9$	D. $500 - p = 184$	
H. $p + 3000 = 10,000$	X. $\frac{x}{7} = 9$	E. $14x = 280$	U. $999 = 3 f$
I. $2q = 128$	Y. $2004 = \frac{1}{2} p$	G. $\frac{1}{3}s = 101$	V. $2000 - r = 994$
J. $z - -6 = 35$	Z. $5f = 75$	H. $107 = \frac{x}{7}$	W. $63 = \frac{1}{3}n$
L. $\frac{m}{3} = 4$	BB. $400 - k = 25$	K. $10,000 - 480 = d$	AA. $11 z = 605$
M. $2r = 1850$	EE. $2 q = 130$	L. $5c = 75, 050$	CC. $-42 - -113 = b$
P. $k - 5 = 55, 000$	FF. $176 \div 11 = w$	N. $140 - -159 = g$	DD. $a + 14 = 70$
R. $\frac{x}{3} = 33$	GG. $x + x = 128$	O. $100 - w = 41$	
S. $4p = 84$			

Name

LOST & FOUND

Matt got so wrapped up in his picture-taking that he wandered off the trail. Now he is totally lost in the woods. The solutions to these equations are lost in the woods, too.

Search the woods to find the correct solution for each equation. Show all the steps as you solve the equation.

1. $9 + 12x = 81$

    x = ____

2. $31 = 8g - 9$

    ____ = g

3. $2r + 5 = 21$

    r = ____

4. $(3 + p)22 = 88$

    p = ____

5. $56 = 8(s - 6)$

    ____ = s

6. $40 = c + 2c - 101$

    ____ = c

7. $4x + x - 2x + 3 = 54$

    x = ____

8. $2(n + 3)/2 = 23$

    n = ____

9. $134 = 7k - 10 + 5k$

    ____ = k

10. $3z + 22 - z = 162$

    z = ____

11. $20 = \dfrac{m + 4}{9}$

    ____ = m

12. $b + 3(b - 4) = 48$

    b = ____

Name

MAKING TRACKS

While wandering through a cave, Chad came face to face with the creature who called the cave "home." Find the path Chad followed as he escaped from the cave by finding the equations that are solved correctly. If the right solution is shown, color the box. Connect the colored boxes to show Chad's path.

Grrrrrr

A. 3y + 13 = -20
y = -11

B. 5p - 4 = 31
p = -7

C. 200 = n + 310
n = -110

D. -7r = 84
r = -12

E. -2 + 8w = 30
w = 4

F. 3.6 + -7 = y
-3.4 = y

G. 5 + 3q = 50
q = 15

H. s + 2s = -42
s = 14

I. 8(c-4) = -16
c = 2

J. 8(c + 2) = 16
c = 2

K. g = 2(10 - 4)
g = 16

L. x + -2 = 33
x = 35

M. s + s = 100 - 10
s = 110

N. 3(x + 6) = 78
x = 20

O. -8m + 2 = 482
m = -60

Name

CLIMBING SOLUTIONS

Scale the rock wall along with Mike and Basha by solving the equations they encounter as they climb.

8. $d + ⅚ = 7$

$d =$ _____

7. $1.5 = x - 6$

_____ $= x$

6. $3p = 0.6$

$p =$ _____

5. $¾ = 20$

$b =$ _____

4. $3n = 4.5$

$n =$ _____

3. $1½ q = 9$

$q =$ _____

2. $-⅖ = -20$

$z =$ _____

1. $6a = 180$

$a =$ _____

8. $\dfrac{8p + 12}{2} = 50$

$p =$ _____

7. $s - ½s + s = 18$

$s =$ _____

6. $1.8 = 9m$

$m =$ _____

5. $⅖ = 6.5$

$p =$ _____

4. $26 = ¼z - 14$

$z =$ _____

3. $3w = -333$

$w =$ _____

2. $\dfrac{m + 3}{5} = 7$

$m =$ _____

1. $35 = y + .003$

$y =$ _____

ELEPHANT FOOT HILL

Name _____

CONFUSION AT THE CROSSROADS

"How much farther is Cripple Creek beyond Razor Rock?" Chad wonders. He's standing at the junction of many paths, trying to calculate some hiking distances. Examine these equations to see if Chad did his calculations right. Use the distances and letter symbols on the signs. Decide if each written equation is true. Write yes or no in front of each equation.

_____ A. $a = 2h$

_____ B. $c - r + f = 1.1$

_____ C. $s/10 = 0.45$

_____ D. $2c + 4 = 10$

_____ E. $2(d + 1.5) = g$

_____ F. $b + g - 3 = 8.2$

_____ G. $m + f + 1.6 = p$

_____ H. $a + s = c + d$

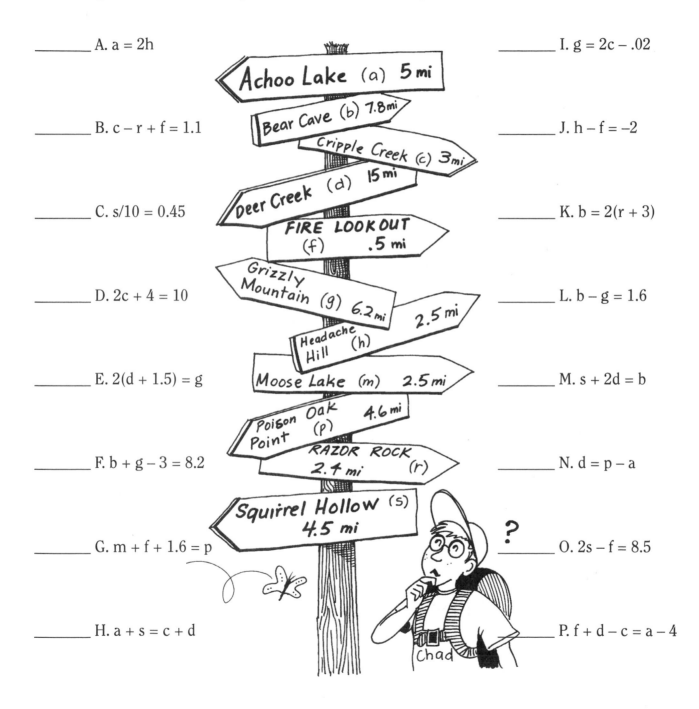

Achoo Lake (a) 5 mi
Bear Cave (b) 7.8 mi
Cripple Creek (c) 3 mi
Deer Creek (d) 15 mi
FIRE LOOKOUT (f) .5 mi
Grizzly Mountain (g) 6.2 mi
Headache Hill (h) 2.5 mi
Moose Lake (m) 2.5 mi
Poison Oak Point (p) 4.6 mi
RAZOR ROCK (r) 2.4 mi
Squirrel Hollow (s) 4.5 mi

Chad

_____ I. $g = 2c - .02$

_____ J. $h - f = -2$

_____ K. $b = 2(r + 3)$

_____ L. $b - g = 1.6$

_____ M. $s + 2d = b$

_____ N. $d = p - a$

_____ O. $2s - f = 8.5$

_____ P. $f + d - c = a - 4$

Name

Basic Skills/Pre-Algebra 6-8+

CULINARY MATTERS

Dig your fork (or your calculator) into these tasty problems about camping food. Write an equation to find the solution to each culinary problem.

1. Mike's stomach is a negative 6 when it comes to pancakes.
    It needs 6 pancakes to fill up.
    Mike eats 12 more than the amount needed to fill the stomach.

    How many pancakes does he eat? _____

2. Zoey ate 14½ pancakes.
    That's 6½ more than her stomach needed.
    How many did her stomach need? _____

3. Mike and Toni ate the same number of bags of gorp.
    This was 3 less than twice what Chad ate.
    Chad ate 5.

    How many bags of gorp did Mike and Toni each eat?_____

4. Matt's two water bottles were filled with 32 ounces each.
    At the end of the day, 7 ounces of water were left.

    How much did he drink? _____

5. Some critters got into the oatmeal. They ate 3 packages of Mike's, 2 of Chad's, and 6 of Matt's. Toni lost ½ as much as the others combined.

    How much of Toni's oatmeal did the critters eat? _____

6. Four campers left 18 chocolate bars in the sun.
    Yolanda lost 4. Sam lost 2 less than Yolanda.
    Chad lost twice what Sam lost.

    How many of Toni's chocolate bars melted? _____

7. Sam brought 3 more cans of stew than Basha, who brought 9.
    The two of them shared their stew with 2 other people.

    If each ate the same amount, how many cans of stew did each person get? _____

8. The group made 30 s'mores. Sam and Basha each ate 3.
    The rest were eaten (equally) by the other 6 campers.

    How many did each of the others eat? _____

Name _____

COOL COMPUTATIONS

There's nothing like the waters of a cool lake to soothe the hot, tired hiker at the end of a long day. Basha and the other campers are content to lie back and float, or dive and swim in Lake Achoo.

Use your problem-solving skills to find the answers to some of their water questions.

Write an equation to find the solution for each problem.

Look out below!

1. Basha's floating time is 15 minutes longer than Zoey's. Together, they float a total of 75 minutes. How long did Zoey float *(f)*?

   f = _____

2. Chad dives off a rock 4.6 ft above the surface. His dive takes him 8.3 ft below the water's surface. How much distance does he cover in the dive *(d)*?

   d = _____

3. Sam's dive covers 6.1 ft total. It began 4.3 ft above the surface. What distance did he travel below the surface *(d)*?

   d = _____

4. Mike can hold his breath for 72 sec. Yolanda can hold hers 26 seconds longer than ½ of Mike's time. How long does Yolanda hold her breath *(t)*?

   t = _____

5. Matt swam up the river. Toni followed him, swimming 31 ft less than ten times as far as Matt. Toni swam 469 ft. What distance did Matt swim *(d)*?

   d = _____

6. While snorkeling around the lake, Toni counted some fish. Mike counted 2 more than Toni. Basha counted 4 times the number seen by Mike and Toni combined. All together they counted 70 fish. Use *(f)* for the variable.

   How many did Toni see? _____

   How many did Mike see? _____

   How many did Basha see? _____

7. The temperature in the lake dropped 2° for each 10 ft below the surface. If the temperature was 70° at the surface, what is the temperature 40 ft below *(t)*?

   t = _____

Name _____

GHOSTLY INEQUALITIES

Basha told a ghost story. It went on for 45 minutes. Matt told a story, too.

His was not as long as Basha's.

This inequality describes Matt's story.
x < 45 and > 0

There are several possible solutions.
48 and –5 would not be solutions.

> < means less than
> \> means greater than
> ≤ means equal to or less than
> ≥ means equal to or greater than

For each inequality, circle the numbers that are solutions.

1. $x \geq 4$	6	–4	4	–2	0
2. $x \leq -1$	4	2	–1	14	6
3. $x > -8$	–8	–10	–6	–2	7
4. $x + 4 < 9$	8	5	–5	3	–2
5. $4x > -12$	–12	6	–3	–5	0
6. $x - 4 \geq 7$	11	–4	6	9	10
7. $\frac{1}{2}x < 2$	4	–4	3	9	–6
8. $3x > -9$	–4	–3	3	–2	0
9. $\frac{1}{4}x < 8$	7	16	20	–5	60
10. $4x + 2 \leq 7$	2	–1	3	–4	–6

Write an inequality for each of these.
Use *x* as the variable.

11. A number is increased by 10.
     The result is greater than 18.

12. 6 is added to 3 times a number.
     The result is less than or equal to 2.

_____

_____

Name

NOISES IN THE NIGHT

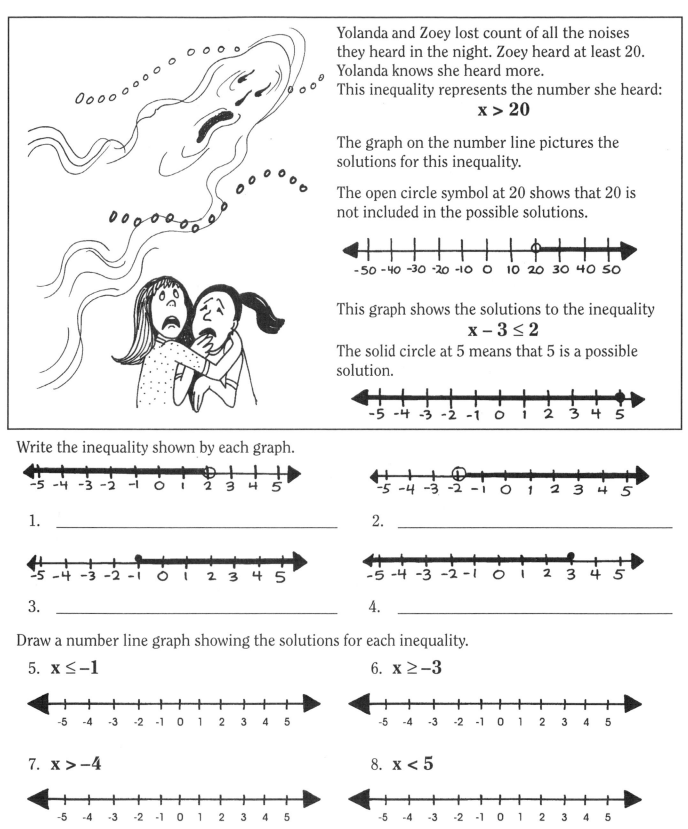

Yolanda and Zoey lost count of all the noises they heard in the night. Zoey heard at least 20. Yolanda knows she heard more.
This inequality represents the number she heard:

x > 20

The graph on the number line pictures the solutions for this inequality.

The open circle symbol at 20 shows that 20 is not included in the possible solutions.

This graph shows the solutions to the inequality

x − 3 ≤ 2

The solid circle at 5 means that 5 is a possible solution.

Write the inequality shown by each graph.

1. _____

2. _____

3. _____

4. _____

Draw a number line graph showing the solutions for each inequality.

5. **x ≤ −1**

6. **x ≥ −3**

7. **x > −4**

8. **x < 5**

Name _____

POISON IVY PROBLEMS

Chad and Zoey are covered with poison ivy. They're trying to cover all the spots on their bodies with soothing aloe lotion. Chad has 5 times as many spots as Zoey. How many does Chad have? You can't figure that out until you know the number of spots on Zoey.

The equation that represents this problem is **x = 5y**.
(x for Chad; y for Zoey)

This problem has two variables. The second one depends on the first.

Complete the table to show some possible solutions.

Complete Tables B-E to show possible solutions for the equations.

A

x = 5y		
x	y	(x, y)
40	8	(40, 8)
10		
5		
0		
–30		
–35		

B

x + 5 = y		
x	y	(x, y)
–3	2	(–3, 2)
–1		
0		
1		
2		
3		

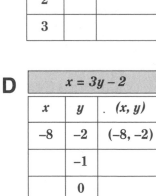

C

x = 2y		
x	y	(x, y)
4	2	(4, 2)
–2		
0		
2		
4		
6		

D

x = 3y – 2		
x	y	(x, y)
–8	–2	(–8, –2)
	–1	
	0	
	1	
	2	
	3	

E

3x = y		
x	y	(x, y)
–5	–15	(–5, –15)
–3		
–1		
0		
2		
5		

Name

SCRAPES, BUMPS, & BRUISES

The numbers of cuts and scrapes, bruises and bumps, and blisters and bites are growing daily. Together, Basha and Matt have 14 bandaged cuts. How many does each of them have? You cannot find out unless you know the number for one of the campers.

This problem can be solved with an equation that has two variables.

The equation that represents this problem is $x + y = 14$. (x for Basha; y for Matt)
Complete the table to show some possible solutions.

A

$x + y = 14$		
x	y	(x, y)
2	12	(2, 12)
4		
5		
8		
10		
12		

1. If Basha has 7, what number does Matt have? _____

2. If Yolanda and Mike have 22 cuts between them, how many does Yolanda *(y)* have if Mike *(x)* has 7? _____

Complete Tables B-E to show possible solutions for the equations.

B

$x = y + 3$		
x	y	(x, y)
–5	–8	(–5, –8)
	0	
	–3	
–2		
5		
	–4	

C

$y = -4x$		
x	y	(x, y)
–3	12	(–3, 12)
	–8	
–1		
4		
	20	
7		

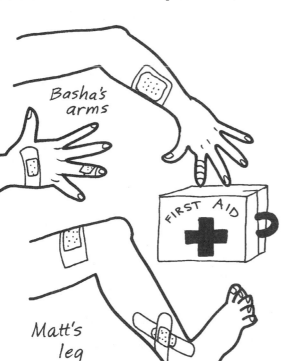

Basha's arms

Matt's leg

FIRST AID

D

$2x + y = 3$		
x	y	(x, y)
–5	13	(–5, 13)
–3		
–1		
0		
3		
6		

E

$x - 2y = 6$		
x	y	(x, y)
0	–3	(0, –3)
	–1	
	0	
	2	
	4	
	5	

Name _____

CREATURE COORDINATES

Bugs are a fact of life on a camping trip. Lightning bugs, beetles, spiders, mosquitoes, and other critters keep the campers company.

Find the location of the creatures on the coordinate grid. Write an ordered pair of numbers to show the location (coordinates) for each bug.

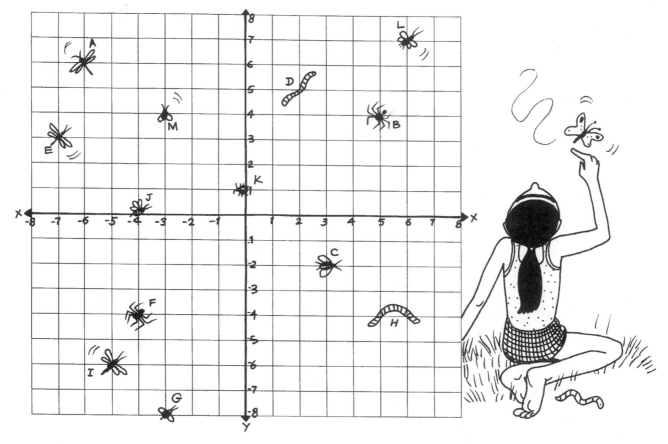

Write an ordered pair for each.

1. A _____
2. B _____
3. C _____
4. D _____
5. E _____
6. F _____
7. G _____

Write the letter.

8. What creature is at (6, 7)?

    _____

9. What creature is at (–4, 0)?

    _____

10. What creature is at (5, –4 and 6, –4)?

    _____

11. What creature is at (–5, –6)?

    _____

12. What creature is at (0, 1)?

    _____

Draw a creature at each of these locations:

13. a spider at (5, 0)
14. a fly at (–8, –8)
15. a dragonfly at (0, –6)
16. a mosquito at (–7, –2)
17. a spider at (–2, 6)
18. a worm at (4, –7)
19. a fly at (–6, –2)
20. a bee at (–1, –2)

Name

A STARTLING MEETING

Mike has met an unexpected visitor! What creature has he stumbled upon?
To find out, follow the directions to plot points and draw lines on the coordinate grid.

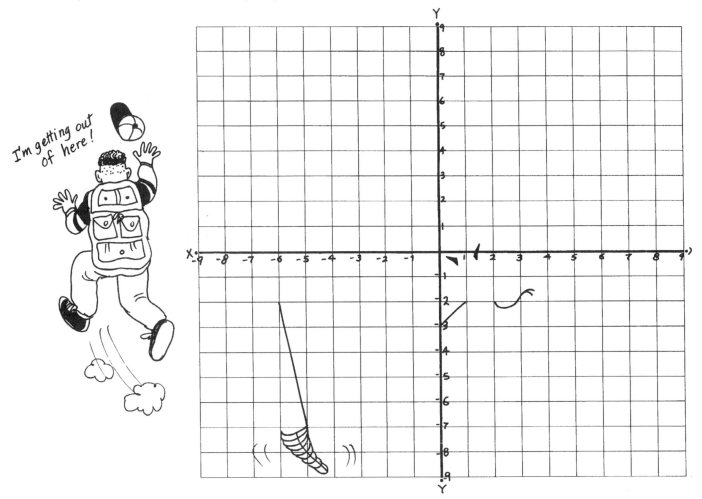

Plot the points in the first three columns.
When the points are plotted, connect them in the order given.

(0, –2)	(0, 4)	(8, 2)
(1, –4)	(–4, 3)	(6, 6)
(4, –2)	(–6, –2)	(2, 8)
(2, 2)	(–3, –7)	(0, 8)
(–2, 1)	(0, –9)	(–4, 6)
(–3, –2)	(2, –9)	(–6, 4)
(–2, –3)	(4, –8)	(–8, –1)
(1, –6)	(5, –7)	(–8, –4)
(6, –2)	(7, –5)	(–6, –7)
(4, 4)	(9, –3)	Stop.
Continue to the next column.	Continue to the next column.	Connect the points.

Plot these points.
Connect them in the
order given.
(0, –1)
(2, –2)
(2.5, 0)
(1, 1)
(0, 1.5)
(–2, –2)
(–2, –3)
Stop.
Connect the points.

Name

LINEAR CONTEMPLATIONS

$y = x + 2$		
x	y	(x, y)
-4	-2	(-4, -2)
-3	-1	(-3, -1)
-2	0	(-2, 0)
-1	1	(-1, 1)
0	2	(0, 2)
1	3	(1, 3)
2	4	(2, 4)

Mike has had no bites for hours, so he's fallen asleep contemplating the possibilities for his fishing line. Which hook in the graph is attached to Mike's line? You can find out by graphing the linear equation.

Graph the solutions shown on the table.
Connect the solutions with a line.
This will show which hook is attached to Mike's fishing line.

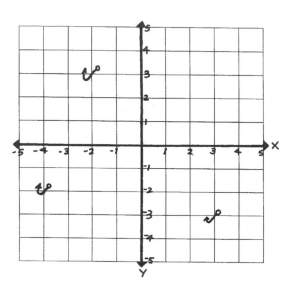

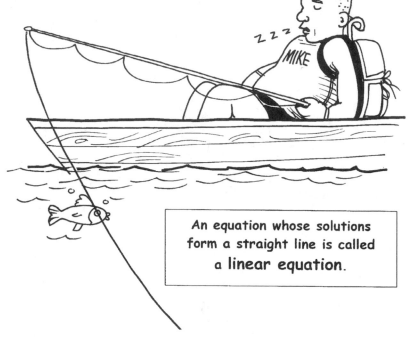

An equation whose solutions form a straight line is called a **linear equation**.

Complete the tables to find solutions for the linear equations on this page and the next page (pages 44 and 45). Then graph each equation to find the right hook for each line.

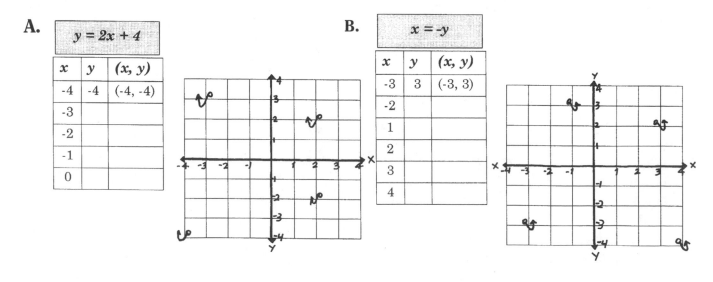

A.

$y = 2x + 4$		
x	y	(x, y)
-4	-4	(-4, -4)
-3		
-2		
-1		
0		

B.

$x = -y$		
x	y	(x, y)
-3	3	(-3, 3)
-2		
1		
2		
3		
4		

Name

LINEAR CONTEMPLATIONS, CONT.

Graph each "fishing line" equation. Draw a hook at the lower end.

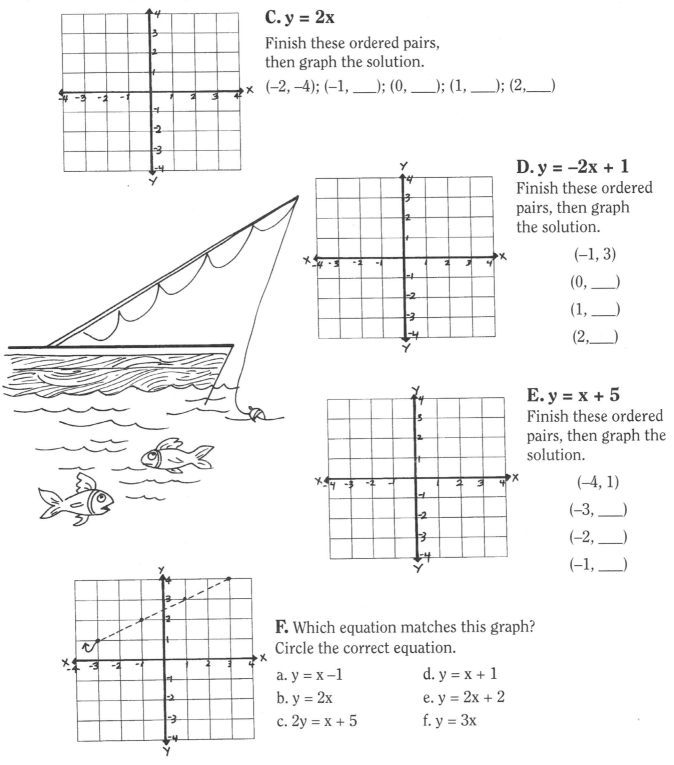

C. y = 2x

Finish these ordered pairs, then graph the solution.

(–2, –4); (–1, ___); (0, ___); (1, ___); (2, ___)

D. y = –2x + 1

Finish these ordered pairs, then graph the solution.

(–1, 3)

(0, ___)

(1, ___)

(2, ___)

E. y = x + 5

Finish these ordered pairs, then graph the solution.

(–4, 1)

(–3, ___)

(–2, ___)

(–1, ___)

F. Which equation matches this graph? Circle the correct equation.

a. y = x –1   d. y = x + 1

b. y = 2x   e. y = 2x + 2

c. 2y = x + 5   f. y = 3x

Name _____

SLIDES, FLIPS, & TURNS

Reflections are exact opposites, or flips, of a figure. They are one kind of transformation to know and use. Slides and turns are the other two.

A figure can be moved on a coordinate plane.

For each point of a figure, there is a corresponding point in the moved (transformed) figure.

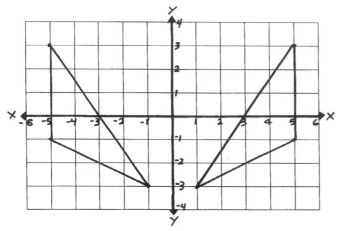

This shows a triangle and its reflection.

For each point on the first triangle, write its corresponding point on the flipped (reflected) figure.

1. (–5, 3) corresponds to _____ .

2. (–5, –1) corresponds to _____ .

3. (–1, –3) corresponds to _____ .

This is a translation (slide) of a rectangle.

For each point on the rectangle, write its corresponding point on the translated rectangle.

4. (–2, 7) corresponds to _____

5. _____ corresponds to _____

6. _____ corresponds to _____

7. _____ corresponds to _____

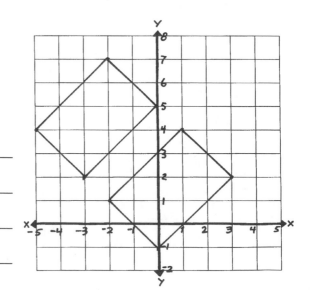

Name

SLIDES, FLIPS, & TURNS, CONT.

Identify the transformation for each pair of figures.
Write S for slide (translation), F for flip (reflection) or T for turn (rotation).

8. _____ 9. _____ 10. _____

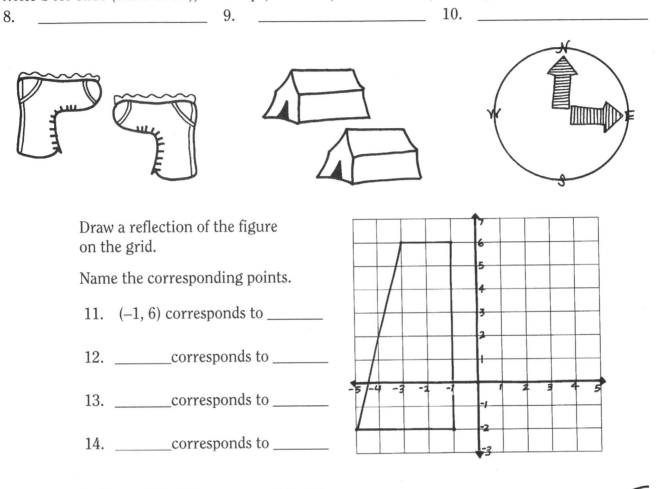

Draw a reflection of the figure
on the grid.

Name the corresponding points.

11. (−1, 6) corresponds to _____

12. _____ corresponds to _____

13. _____ corresponds to _____

14. _____ corresponds to _____

On this grid, draw a slide, flip, or turn of the hiker.

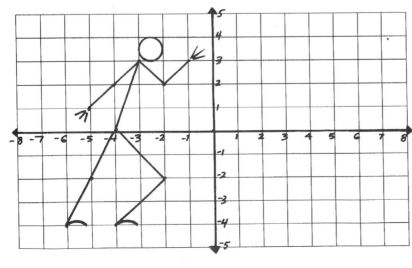

What a handsome guy!

CLOUD-WATCHING

Yolanda gazes up at a sky filled with unusual cloud patterns.
This is what she sees when she studies the clouds.

Find the pattern.

Draw the next two cloud formations to continue the pattern.

Study these sequence to predict the patterns.
Complete the next two figures in the sequence.

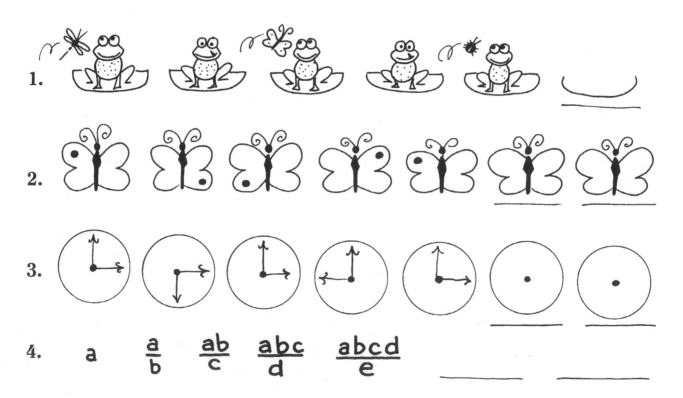

Name _____

CLOUD-WATCHING, CONT.

Find the patterns.

Use them to predict the next one, two, or three figures in each sequence.

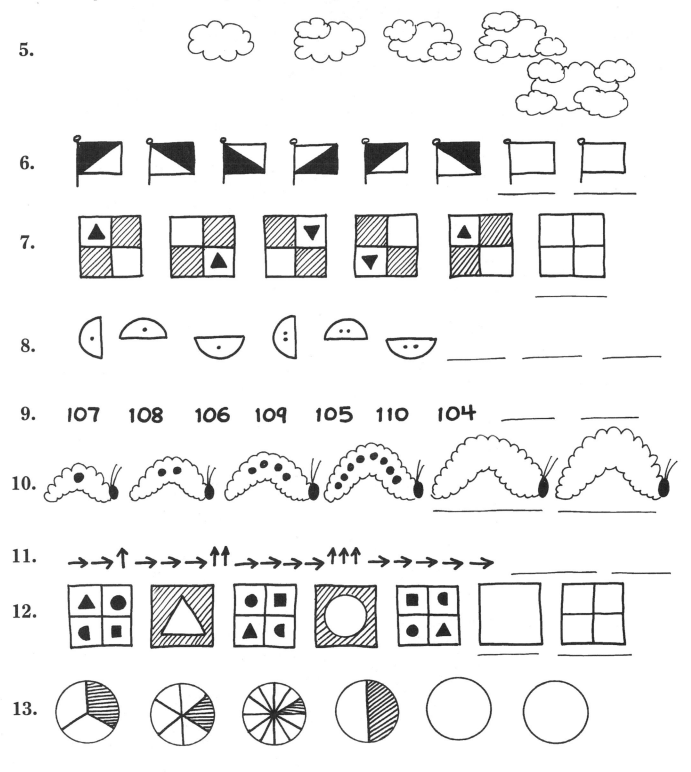

9. 107   108   106   109   105   110   104 ___ ___ ___

THE END OF THE TRAIL

Write a proportion to show the relationship between the numbers in these problems from the last day on the trail. Use x as the unknown number in the proportion.

Then solve each proportion.

1. On the last day, the hikers covered 4.5 miles in 2 hours. If the total walking time was 6 hours, and they walked at the same rate all day, how long was the trail?

Answer: _____

2. Mike took 21 pictures with his camera in the first 3 hours on the trail. He continued his picture-taking at the same rate through the whole hike. How much time had passed when he'd taken 35 pictures?

Answer: _____

3. Toni drank 0.75 quarts of water in the first 3 miles of the trail. At this rate, how much will she drink in 13 miles?

Answer: _____

4. Matt rested 15 times in 5 hours. He rested at the same rate throughout his hike. How many times did he rest in 3 hours?

Answer: _____

5. The group ate 9 bags of gorp on their way out of the wilderness area. Their hike was 6 hours long. Assuming that they ate at the same rate throughout the hike, how much time did it take to eat 6 bags of gorp?

Answer: _____

Solve these proportions.

6. $\frac{n}{12} = \frac{5}{15}$

   n = _____

7. $\frac{12}{n} = \frac{72}{108}$

   n = _____

Name _____

APPENDIX

CONTENTS

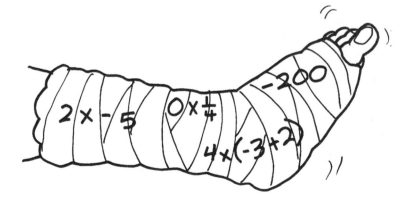

GLOSSARY OF PRE-ALGEBRA TERMS

Absolute Value—The distance of a number from zero on a number line

Associative Property—A property stating that changing the grouping of numbers does not change the sum or product

Axes—The two perpendicular number lines in a coordinate plane that intersect at 0

Coefficient—The number of a variable: In the term 6.5 x, 6.5 is the coefficient of x.

Coincide—When two lines intersect in more than one point, they coincide.

Collinear Points—Points that lie on the same line

Commutative Property—A property stating that changing the order of the numbers does not change the sum or product

Coordinate—A number paired with a point

Coordinates—A pair of numbers paired with a point

Coordinate Plane—A grid on a plane with two perpendicular number lines (axes)

Coplanar—Lines or points in the same plane

Distributive Property—A property stating that the product of a factor and a sum is equal to the sum of the products

Equation—A number sentence that states that two numbers or quantities are equal

Equivalent Equations—Equations that have the same solution

Evaluate—To substitute a number for each variable in an expression and simplify the expression

Function—A set of ordered pairs (x, y) where for each value of x there is only one value of y

Graph of an Equation—All the points in a coordinate plane whose coordinates satisfy the equation

Graph of an Integer—A point paired with a number on a number line

Identity Properties—Properties that state that the sum of 0 and any number is that number, and that the product of 1 and any number is that number

Inequality—A number sentence that states that two numbers or quantities are not equal

Intersecting Lines—Lines that cross each other

Inverse Operation—The opposite operation that "undoes" another

Irrational Number—A number that is not rational: a nonterminating and nonrepeating decimal

Like Terms—Terms that have the same variable

Line—A set of points that extends without end in opposite directions

Linear Equation—An equation whose graph is a straight line

Negative Numbers—Numbers less than zero

Number Line—A line in which points have been paired with numbers

Number Sentence—A sentence showing a relationship among numbers

Open Sentences—Number sentences that contain variables

Opposites—Two numbers on a number line that are the same distance from zero on opposite sides

Opposites Properties—Properties that state that subtracting a number is the opposite operation of adding that number, and dividing by a number is the opposite operation of multiplying by that number

Ordered Pair—A pair of numbers in which the order shows the location of a point on a grid: (6, 8) is an ordered pair

Origin—The point where the x-axis and the y-axis intersect on a grid

Point—An exact location

Positive Numbers—Numbers greater than zero

Proportion—An equation which states that two ratios are equal

Quadrant—One of the four sections in a coordinate plane formed by the x and y axes

Radical Sign—The symbol showing the positive square root: $\sqrt{}$

Rational Number—Any number that can be written as the quotient of two integers where the denominator is not zero. The number can be written as a fraction, decimal, repeating decimal, or terminating decimal.

Real Number—Any rational or irrational number

Reflection—The transformation of a geometric figure where the figure changes position through the motion of a flip

Rotation—The transformation of a geometric figure where the figure changes position where the figure changes position through the motion of a turn

Solution—The number that replaces the variable in an equation to make the equation true

Solution of a System—An ordered pair that is a solution of both equations in a system

System of Equations—Two equations that have the same variables

Terms—The variables and numbers in a mathematical expression that are joined by signs for operations

Translation—The transformation of a geometric figure where the figure changes position through the motion of a slide

Variable—A letter used to represent a number in a mathematical expression

Unlike Terms—Terms that do not have the same variable

x-axis—The horizontal number line in a coordinate plane

y-axis—The vertical number line in a coordinate plane

Zero Property of Multiplication—The property stating that the product of 0 and any number is 0.

TIPS FOR SOLVING EQUATIONS

Remember these tips about integers:

Addition: The sum of two positive integers will be a positive integer. The sum of two negative integers will be a negative integer.

Subtraction: To subtract an integer, add its opposite.

Multiplication: The product of a positive number and a negative number is a negative number. The product of two positive or two negative numbers is a positive number.

Division: The quotient of two positive integers or two negative integers is a positive integer. The quotient of a positive integer and a negative integer is a negative integer.

Simplify the expression to make the solution easier:

$3x + 17 - 12 = 11$ . . . . .simplify to: $3x + 5 = 11$

$4(b + 5) - b = 23$ . . . . .simplify to: $3b + 20 = 23$

Use inverse operations to get the variable alone on one side of the equation:

A. $\quad 36 = t - 9$ $\qquad$ Add 9 to both sides.

$\quad 36 + 9 = t - 9 + 9$

$\quad 36 + 9 = t$

$\quad 45 = t$

B. $\quad 2x + 20 = 48$

$\quad 2x + 20 - 20 = 48 - 20$ $\qquad$ Subtract 20 from both sides.

$\quad 2x = 28$

$\quad \frac{2x}{2} = \frac{28}{2}$ $\qquad$ Divide both sides by 2.

$\quad x = 14$

To solve equations with more than one step:

$\qquad\qquad\qquad\qquad 7a + 8a - 5 = 145$

1. Simplify the equation.

$\qquad\qquad\qquad\qquad 15a - 5 = 145$

2. Rewrite so the term with the variable is alone on one side. Use inverse operations.

$\qquad\qquad\qquad\qquad 15a - 5 + 5 = 145 + 5$

3. Use inverse operations to get the variable to a single number.

$\qquad\qquad\qquad\qquad 15a / 15 = 150/15$

4. Solve.

$\qquad\qquad\qquad\qquad a = 10$

NUMBER PROPERTIES

The Associative Property for Addition
The way in which the numbers are grouped does not affect the sum.

$(a + b) + c = a + (b + c)$ $(19 + 6) + 20 = 19 + (6 + 20)$

The Associative Property for Multiplication
The way in which the numbers are grouped does not affect the product.

$(a \times b) \times c = a \times (b \times c)$ $(5 \times 3) \times 10 = 5 \times (3 \times 10)$

The Commutative Property for Addition
The order in which the numbers are added does not affect the sum.

$a + b = b + a$ $6 + -4 = -4 + 6$

The Commutative Property for Multiplication
The order in which the numbers are multiplied does not affect the product.

$a \times b = b \times a$ $30 \times 5 = 5 \times 30$

The Distributive Property
To multiply a sum, first add, and then multiply.
Or multiply the addends separately, and then add.

$a \times (b + c) = a \times b + a \times c$

$-8 \times (5 + 3) = -8 \times 8 = -64$ OR $-8 \times (5 + 3) = -8 \times 5 + -8 \times 3$

The Identity Properties
The sum of zero and any number is that number.

$0 + a = a$ $0 + 14 = 14$ $0 + -60 = -60$

The product of one and any number is that number

$1 \times a = a$ $1 \times 24 = 24$ $1 \times -13 = -13$

The Property of Zero
The product of zero and any number is zero.

$0 \times a = 0$ $0 \times 52 = 0$ $0 \times -9 = 0$

The Opposites Property
Subtracting a number is the opposite of adding that number.

Dividing by a number is the opposite of multiplying by that number.

$4 - -5 = 9$ $-24 \div 6 = -4$ $-4 \times 6 = -24$

PRE-ALGEBRA
SKILLS TEST

Questions 1–10. For each definition, choose a matching term from the sign. Write the term on the line.

• absolute values
• integers
• coordinates
• origin
• reflection
• variable
• translation
• solution
• linear equation
• terms
• expression

Mt. Grizzly

_____ 1. A number that replaces the variable in an equation to make the equation true.

_____ 2. The point where the x-axis and the y-axis intersect on a grid.

_____ 3. A sentence that uses mathematical symbols instead of words.

_____ 4. The distance of a number from zero on a number line.

_____ 5. The variables and numbers in a mathematical expression.

_____ 6. The transformation of a figure through the motion of a slide.

_____ 7. The transformation of a figure through the motion of a flip.

_____ 8. A letter used to represent a number in a mathematical expression.

_____ 9. An equation whose solutions form a straight line.

_____ 10. Positive numbers (1, 2, 3 . . .), negative numbers (–1, –2, –3, . . .), and zero.

Write the absolute value:

11. $|-7| =$ _____

12. $|34| =$ _____

Write the integers in order from least to greatest:

13. 7, –9, 8, 0, 9, –3

_____

14. 20, –10, –5, 5, 10, –20

_____

Add, subtract, multiply, or divide the integers to find the answer.

15. $-22 + -1 =$ _____

16. $-17 - 4 - -4 =$ _____

17. $-6 \times -4 =$ _____

18. $-300 \div 60 =$ _____

19. $-11 + 14 - -6 =$ _____

20. $(-3 \times 2) \div -6 =$ _____

21. $(20 \times -5) - -100 =$ _____

The temperature was 18°F when the campers went to bed at 10:00 p.m. By 4:00 a.m., it had fallen 22°. By 6:00 a.m., the temperature was –12°F.

22. What was the temperature at 4:00 a.m.? _____

23. How far had the temperature fallen from 10:00 p.m. to 6:00 a.m. the next morning? _____

Choose the mathematical expression that matches each of these descriptions about packing camping supplies.

24. The difference between the weight of two packs (p) and 4 water bottles (w)

    a. 2p – 4w   b. p –4w

    c. 4(w + p) + 2   d. 2p + 4w

Name _____

Basic Skills/Pre-Algebra, 6-8+

25. The weight of three tents (t), increased by twice the sum of weights of a sleeping bag (s) and a frying pan (f).
    a. 3t + 2s + f   b. 3 (t + s + f + 2)
    c. 3t + 2(s + f)   d. 3 + 2 + t + s + f

26. The weight of one pair of boots (b) increased by four cook stoves (c), increased by six pairs of socks (p)
    a. b + 4 (c + 6p)   b. b + 4c +6p
    c. b – 4c + 6s   d. 4(b + c + 6s)

Write a mathematical expression to match each description.

27. Twice the sum of the weights of a tent (t), a sleeping bag (s), and four water bottles (w)

    _____

28. The weight of a pack (p) decreased by the weight of twelve tent stakes (s), two cook pots (c), and a pair of boots (b)

    _____

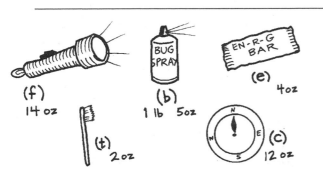

(f) 14 oz   (b) 1 lb 5 oz   (e) 4 oz   (t) 2 oz   (c) 12 oz

Use the information given in the above picture to answer questions 29–32.

Tell whether the expressions are true. Write T (true) or F (false) in front of each expression.

_____ 29. 2 c < 2f

_____ 30. 4e – 2 = f

_____ 31. 10t > b

_____ 32. 2c + b = 3f + t + ¼e

33. How many variables?_____
    $$12x + y - 3y = 42$$

34. How many terms? _____
    $$4p + 9 + p - x + 35x = -7$$

35. What is the coefficient of y? _____
    $$-7x + q - 13y$$

Simplify the expressions.

36. 2(k + 9) + k _____

37. 4z + 6x –7z _____

38. (8g + 72) ÷ 4 _____

39. 12y – 3y + q _____

40. –25 + p –10p _____

Circle the correct equation to match the statement or problem.

41. Toni had 14 fewer bug bites than Yolanda.
    a. t – y = 14
    b. 14t = y
    c. t = y – 14

42. Mike swatted mosquitoes for 2 + hours. He killed 33. How many mosquitoes (m) did he kill (on the average) per hour?
    a. 33 ÷ 2½ = m
    b. 2½ ÷ 33 = m
    c. 33 – 2½ = m

43. Sam had 12 more than three times the number of bites as Chad.
    a. s = c – 12 x 3
    b. s = 3c + 12
    c. c = 2s

44. The seven hikers used three cans of bug spray for the first week. At the end of two weeks, they had used six cans. How many cans (c) did they use the second week?
    a. 7 + c = 2 + 6
    b. 3 + x = 6
    c. 3 (6 + x) = 7

Rewrite each equation using inverse operations.

45. p + 200 = –100

    _____

46. –50 + p = 13

    _____

47. –5 = t + 9

    _____

Name _____

Write an equation to match each statement or problem.

48. The campfire burned for an hour less than twice as long on Thursday night (t) as it burned on Wednesday night (w).

_____

49. Sam gathered 38 pieces of firewood. Together he and Matt gathered 50. How many did Matt find?

_____

50. The campers toasted 4 bags of marshmallows. One bag had 25. The other bags had a different number, equal to each other. They toasted a total of 119 marshmallows. How many were in each of the other bags?

_____

Tell if each equation is solved correctly. Write yes or no.

_____ 51. $0.9 + x = 0.18$
                         $x = 0.27$

_____ 52. $\frac{1}{2} + y - 15\frac{1}{4} = 4\frac{1}{4}$
                         $y = -20$

_____ 53. $6 (p + 12) = 2$
                         $p = 10$

Solve these equations.

54. $\frac{x - 37}{3} = 21$
           $x =$ _____

55. $g + -25 = 225$
           $g =$ _____

Write the property used to solve each equation. Use the first letter.

    (A) Associative Propery
    (I) Identity Property
    (C) Commutative Property
    (D) Distributive Property
    (Z) Zero Property
    (O) Opposites Property

_____ 56. $-35 \times 1 = -35$

_____ 57. $-3 + (12 + 6) = (-3 + 12) + 6$

_____ 58. $20 \times -7 = -7 \times 20$

_____ 59. $4 \times (5 + 9) = 4 \times 5 + 4 \times 9$

_____ 60. $0 \times -200 = 0$

Solve these equations:

61. $100 = -4n$
           $n =$ _____

62. $13 p = -39$
           $p =$ _____

63. $\frac{s}{8} = 16$
           $s =$ _____

Solve these equations.

64. $67.5 = 7.5n$
           $n =$ _____

65. $7b + 8 - 2b = 48$
                    $b =$ _____

66. $-8.2 s + 3s = 20.8$
                    $s =$ _____

67. Which inequality matches this graph? Circle one.

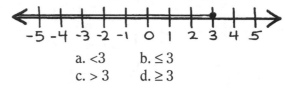

    a. <3 b. ≤ 3
    c. > 3 d. ≥ 3

Write the inequality shown by each graph.

68.

_____

69.

_____

70.

_____

71. Is $(-3, 8)$ a solution to the equation $x + y = 5$? _____

72. Is $(-3, 9)$ a solution to the equation $2x + y = 3$? _____

73. Is $(-13, -17)$ a solution to the equation $y = x + 4$? _____

Name

Basic Skills/Pre-Algebra, 6-8+   Copyright ©2000 by Incentive Publications, Inc., Nashville, TN.

Is there a poison ivy leaf at each of these locations? Write yes or no.

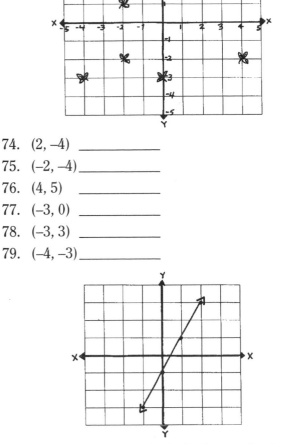

74. (2, –4) _____

75. (–2, –4)_____

76. (4, 5) _____

77. (–3, 0) _____

78. (–3, 3) _____

79. (–4, –3)_____

80. The above is a graph of which equation? _____

    a. y = x – 1   c. y = 2x –1

    b. y = x + 1   d. y = 2x

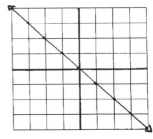

81. The above is a graph of which equation? _____

    a. x = y   c. 2x = y

    b. y = -x   d. y = –2x

Which transformation is shown? Write *slide*, *flip*, or *turn*.

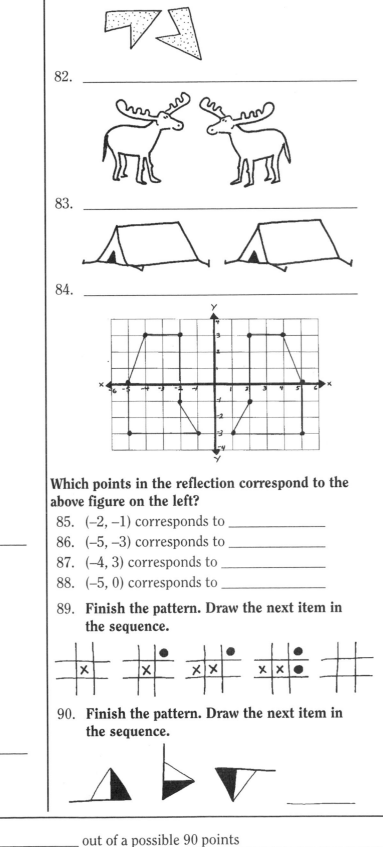

82. _____

83. _____

84. _____

Which points in the reflection correspond to the above figure on the left?

85. (–2, –1) corresponds to _____

86. (–5, –3) corresponds to _____

87. (–4, 3) corresponds to _____

88. (–5, 0) corresponds to _____

89. **Finish the pattern. Draw the next item in the sequence.**

90. **Finish the pattern. Draw the next item in the sequence.**

SCORE: Total Points _____ out of a possible 90 points

Name _____

Pre-Algebra
SKILLS TEST ANSWER KEY

1. solution	33. 2	65. 8
2. origin	34. 4	66. 4
3. expression	35. 13	67. b
4. absolute value	36. $3k + 18$	68. > -1
5. terms	37. $-3z + 6x$	69. ≥ -2
6. translation	38. $2g + 18$	70. < 2
7. reflection	39. $9y + q$	71. yes
8. variable	40. $-25 - 9p$	72. yes
9. linear equation	41. c	73. no
10. integers	42. a	74. no
11. 7	43. b	75. no
12. 34	44. b	76. yes
13. $-9, -7, -3, 0, 8, 9$	45. $p + 200 - 200 = -100 - 200$	77. no
14. $-20, -10, -5, 5, 10, 20$	46. $-50 + 50 + p = 13 + 50$	78. yes
15. -23	47. $-5 - 9 = t + 9 - 9$	79. yes
16. -17	48. $t = 2w - 1$	80. c
17. 24	49. $38 + x = 50$	81. b
18. -50	50. $25 + 3x = 119$	82. turn
19. 9	51. no	83. flip
20. 1	52. no	84. slide
21. 0	53. no	85. $(2, -1)$
22. $-4°$	54. 100	86. $(5, -3)$
23. $30°$	55. 250	87. $(4, 3)$
24. a	56. I	88. $(5, 0)$
25. c	57. A	89. Check student drawings to see that they follow the sequence.
26. b	58. C	
27. $2(t + s + 4w)$	59. D	
28. $p - 12s - 2c - b$	60. Z	90. Check student drawings to see that they follow the sequence.
29. T	61. -25	
30. T	62. -3	
31. F	63. -128	
32. T	64. 9	

ANSWERS

page 10

1. a.	P	4. a.	P	7. a.	N
b.	3	b.	5	b.	4
c.	–3	c.	–5	c.	4
2. a.	N	5. a.	P	8. a.	N
b.	2	b.	8	b.	6
c.	2	c.	–8	c.	6
3. a.	P	6. a.	N		
b.	12	b.	7		
c.	–12	c.	7		

page 11

1. 4	11. >
2. 3	12. <
3. 2	13. >
4. 6	14. >
5. 6	15. –7, –6, –4, –2, 3, 5, 8, 12
6. 1	16. –20, –7, –1, 0, 3, 4, 6, 20
7. >	17. –16, –8, –4, –3, 3, 5, 10
8. <	18. –8, –4, –2, 2, 4, 6, 8
9. >	19. –12, –7, 0, 2, 6, 7, 8
10. >	20. –8, –6, 0, 2, 5, 9, 11

page 12

1.	4	7.	0	13.	–22
2.	–15	8.	–75	14.	–8
3.	–99	9.	–19	15.	3
4.	4	10.	–5	16.	–59
5.	–4	11.	–29	17.	42
6.	1	12.	6	18.	–21

page 13

Answer to equation at top of page: 6 miles

1. –10	12. –6
2. 10	13. 3
3. –10	14. –10
4. 10	15. 64
5. –7	16. –11
6. 7	17. 19
7. –7	18. 4
8. 7	19. –4
9. 0	20. –29
10. –4	21. 5.8 miles
11. 23	

page 14

Chart

1.	10°	–15°			
2.	37°	32°	22°	12°	–3°
3.	55°	50°	40°	30°	15°
4.	11°	6°	–4°	–14°	–29°
5.	6°	1°	–9°	–19°	–34°
6.	10°	5°	0°	–10°	–35°

Bottom

7. –70	12. –2500
8. –42	13. 1500
9. 60	14. –200,000
10. –56	15. –320
11. 10,000	16. 630 or 700

page 15

1. Mar	8. Oct
2. Apr	9. –10
3. Nov	10. 13
4. Oct	11. –100
5. Aug	12. 20
6. Nov	13. –4
7. Feb and June	14. –100

page 16

Equations may vary slightly, depending on what arrangement of terms the student chooses. Check to see that equations accurately reflect the problems, and that student has used integers in the equation.

1. –2 + 2 + –3 = –3
   Answer: Shoes, Boots

2. –3 +10 = 7
   Answer: Videos, Slides

3. 2 x –2 = –4
   Answer: Repair Shop

4. –4 + 8 + –1 = 3
   Answer: Clothing

5. 2 – –4 = 6
   Answer: 6

6. –1 + 9 = 8
   Answer: Climbing Gear

7. –3 + 4 + –1 = 0 or –3+ –1 + 4 = 0
   Answer: Sleeping Bags

8. 3 + –3 + 8 + –2 = 6
   Answer: Books & Maps

page 17

1. Toni
2. Mike
3. Basha
4. T
5. blank or F
6. blank or F
7. T
8–12. Answers may vary. Check phrases to make sure they give an accurate statement of a relationship between the two numbers.

page 18

Top questions:
   yes
   t < 2s

1. 3w + 2p
2. 4f + s
3. 2c+10
4. b – 3
5. f < 2t
6. 3(p + b)
7. 5w + 2
8. c + 2w + f < 100

page 19

Expressions may vary slightly, depending on what arrangement of terms the student chooses. Check to see that expressions accurately reflect the statements, and that student has used integers in each expression.

1. m + 3
2. 15 r – 7j
3. 4p – 2n
4. 12g – 4g
5. 8c – 5
6. 2 (2b + 6j)
7. 3 (2s –5f)
8. 10 h + s + 2p
9. 2a < 3p
10. 5 (b + a)
11. ½ r + ¼ g
12. 10(bf)

page 20

1. 2	10. 4
2. 2	11. 4
3. 2	12. 1
4. 4	13. 5
5. L	14. 7z, 18m, ½ b
6. U	coefficient of z is 7
7. U	coefficient of m is 18
8. U	coefficient of b is ½
9. 2	

page 21

Answers may vary, depending upon the order in which student chooses to place the terms of the expression.

1. 8a	11. 2y + 2x
2. 2x	12. 27g – 3s
3. 8k	13. 11m + 100
4. 19 ¼ c	14. 2w + 12
5. 11y – 5	15. 3b + 10
6. ¼ x + 2	16. 7a + 6
7. 7t + 14	17. 16n + 10
8. 3.2k + 5	18. 6x + 3y
9. z + 6x	19. 9p
10. 3n + 4p	20. 3s –2t

page 22

Answers may vary, depending upon the order in which student chooses to place the terms of the expression.

Basic Skills/Pre-Algebra, 6-8+

1. 8y + 7
2. 4x + 35
3. 8p
4. 3x/5
5. 3z + 12
6. 9t + 300
7. 201y + 6
8. 4½b

9. 45 + 7a + 6b
10. –2g + 24
11. b + 2d + c
12. –6x + 12
13. 23p+45
14. –3z –x
15. 99j + x
16. 4j + 6k

page 23

Top correct equation to circle: s = 2t – 3

1. c
2. a
3. a

4. c
5. c
6. c

7. c
8. b
9. a

10. b

page 24

Answers may vary, depending upon the order in which student chooses to place the terms of the equation, and upon the letters chosen to represent the terms.

1. z = 2c + 3
2. t = (m + b) – 5
3. s = 4 (z + t)
4. y = s – 5
5. t = (m + z) – 16
6. s = t + 23

7. b = 18 + z
8. s = f – 3
9. m = ¼t
10. m = 2s – 3
11. m + w = s + t
12. t = 3a – 5

page 25

1. c; 26
2. b; 36
3. b; 4
4. a; 2 ¼
5. b; 33
6. b; 4
7. a; 7

page 26

Equations may vary, depending upon the order in which student chooses to place the terms of the equation, and upon the letters chosen to represent the terms. Answers (solutions to equations), however, should not vary.

1. t = 21 – 14
   Answer: 7 min
2. w = 100 – 30
   Answer: 70 lb
3. d = 280/2 – 20
   Answer: 120 ft
4. 2(3 + 6) = r
   Answer: 18 times
5. m = 50–25
   Answer: 25 min
6. 9 = 2d – 3
   Answer: 6 times
7. p = 208 – 70 – 100
   Answer: 38 lb

page 27

1.
$$x + 8 = 20$$
$$x + 8 - 8 = 20 - 8$$
$$x = 12$$

2.
$$p - 40 = -300$$
$$p - 40 + 40 = -300 + 40$$
$$p = -260$$

3.
$$5c = -35$$
$$5c/5 = -35/5$$
$$c = -7$$

4.
$$y/6 = -8$$
$$y/6 \times 6 = -8 \times 6$$
$$y = -48$$

5.
$$x + 15 = 7$$
$$x + 15 - 15 = 7 - 15$$
$$x = -8$$

6.
$$q - 25 = -15$$
$$q - 25 + 25 = -15 + 25$$
$$q = 10$$

7.
$$7r = -84$$
$$7r/7 = -84/7$$
$$r = -12$$

8.
$$z/7 = -8$$
$$z/7 \times 7 = -8 \times 7$$
$$z = -56$$

page 28

1. Identity
2. Identity
3. Associative
4. Commutative
5. Distributive
6. Distributive
7. Commutative
8. Identity

9. Zero
10. Identity
11. Opposites
12. Associative
13. Opposites
14. Commutative
15. Identity
16. Zero

page 29

1. c
2. b
3. d

4. c
5. b
6. a

7. c
8. d
9. c

10. d
11. c
12. b

page 30

Top question: yes

Correct solutions are 1, 2, 3, 6, 8, 9, 10, 11, 12, 14, 15, 18
Correct answers to wrong solutions are:

4. 5000
5. –36

7. –106
13. –60

16. 1000
17. –2

page 31

Across

A. 46
E. 27
G. 2111
H. 7000
I. 64
J. 29
L. 12

M. 925
P. 55,005
R. 99
S. 21
T. 49
U. 308
V. 111

X. 63
Y. 4008
Z. 15
BB. 375
EE. 65
FF. 16
GG. 64

Down

B. 600
C. 81
D. 316
E. 20
G. 202
H. 749

K. 9520
L. 15,010
N. 299
O. 59
Q. 518
T. 4116

U. 333
V. 1006
W. 189
AA. 55
CC. 71
DD. 56

page 32

1. 6
2. 5
3. 8

4. 1
5. 13
6. 47

7. 17
8. 20
9. 12

10. 70
11. 176
12. 15

page 33

Path should follow these correctly-solved equations. NOTE: Student may connect these equations in a different order than this.

A.
C.
D.
E.
F.

G.
I.
L.
N.
O.

page 34

(left) Mike's path

8. 6 1/6
7. 7.5
6. 0.2
5. 80

4. 1.5
3. 6
2. 100
1. 30

(right) Basha's path

8. 11
7. 12
6. 0.2
5. 32.5

4. 160
3. –111
2. 32
1. 34.997

page 35

A. yes
B. yes
C. yes
D. yes

E. no
F. no
G. yes
H. no

I. no
J. no
K. no
L. yes

M. no
N. no
O. yes
P. no

page 36

The equations shown may not be exactly the equations written by student. Give credit for any equation that accurately reflects and solves the problem. The solutions, however, should not vary.

1. –6 + x = 12
   Answer: 18
2. x = 14 ½ – 6 ½
   Answer: 8
3. x = $\frac{(2 \times 5) - 3}{2}$
   Answer: 3 + bags
4. 2 x 32 – x = 7
   Answer: 57 oz
5. $\frac{3 + 2 + 6}{2}$ = x
   Answer: 5 ½ packages
6. 4 + (4 – 2) +2(4 – 2) + x = 18
   Answer: 8
7. $\frac{9 + (9 + 3)}{4}$ = x
   Answer: 5 ¼ cans
8. $\frac{30 - (3 + 3)}{6}$ = x
   Answer: 4

page 37

The equations shown may not be exactly the equations written by student. Give credit for any equation that accurately reflects and solves the problem. The solutions, however, should not vary.

1. $(f + 15) + f = 75$
   $f = 30$ min

2. $d = 4.6 + 8.3$
   $d = 12.9$ ft

3. $d = 6.1 - 4.3$
   $d = 1.8$ ft

4. $t = 72/2 + 26$
   $t = 62$ sec

5. $10\,d - 31 = 469$
   $d = 50$ ft

6. $f + (f + 2) + 4(f + f + 2) = 70$
   Toni saw 6
   Mike saw 8
   Basha saw 56

7. $t = 70 - (2 \times 4)$
   $t = 62°$

page 38

1. 6, 4	7. –4, 3, –6
2. –1	8. 3, –2, 0
3. –6, –2, 7	9. 7, 16, 20, –5
4. –5, 3, –2	10. –1, –4, –6
5. 6, 0	11. $x + 10 > 18$
6. 11	12. $3x + 6 \leq 2$

page 39

1. $x < 2$
   2. $x > -2$
   3. $x > -1$
   4. $x < 3$
5–8. Check student graphs to see that solutions are shown correctly. 5 and 6 should have solid circles at –1 and –3 respectively. 7 and 8 should have open circles at –8 and 6 respectively.

page 40

A. $x = 10, y = 2, (10, 2)$
   $x = 5, y = 1, (5, 1)$
   $x = 0, y = 0, (0, 0)$
   $x = -30, y = -6, (-30, -6)$
   $x = -35, y = -7, (-35, -7)$

B. $x = -1, y = 4, (-1, 4)$
   $x = 0, y = 5, (0, 5)$
   $x = 1, y = 6, (1, 6)$
   $x = 2, y = 7 (2, 7)$
   $x = 3, y = 8 (3, 8)$

C. $x = 2, y = -1, (-2, -1)$
   $x = 0, y = 0, (0, 0)$
   $x = 2, y = 1, (2, 1)$
   $x = 4, y = 2, (4, 2)$
   $x = 6, y = 3, (6, 3)$

D. $x = -5, y = -1, (-5, -1)$
   $x = -2, y = 0, (-2, 0)$
   $x = 1, y = 1, (1, 1)$
   $x = 4, y = 2, (4, 2)$
   $x = 7, y = 3, (7, 3)$

E. $x = -3, y = -9, (-3, -9)$
   $x = -1, y = -3, (-1, -3)$
   $x = 0, y = 0, (0, 0)$
   $x = 2, y = 6, (2, 6)$
   $x = 5, y = 15, (5, 15)$

page 41

1. 7
2. 15
A. $x = 4, y = 10, (4, 10)$
   $x = 5, y = 9, (5, 9)$
   $x = 8, y = 6, (8, 6)$
   $x = 10, y = 4, (10, 4)$
   $x = 12, y = 2, (12, 2)$

B. $x = 3, y = 0, (3, 0)$
   $x = 0, y = -3, (0, -3)$
   $x = -2, y = -5, (-2, -5)$
   $x = 5, y = 2, (5, 2)$
   $x = -1, y = -4, (-1, -4)$

C. $x = 2, y = -8. (2, -8)$
   $x = -1, y = 4, (-1, 4)$
   $x = 4, y = -16, (4, -16)$
   $x = -5, y = 20, (-5, 20)$
   $x = 7, y = -28, (7, -28)$

D. $x = -3, y = 9, (-3, 9)$
   $x = -1, y = 5, (-1, 5)$
   $x = 0, y = 3, (0, 3)$
   $x = 3, y = -3, (3, -3)$
   $x = 6, y = -9, (6, -9)$

E. $x = 4, y = -1, (4, -1)$
   $x = 6, y = 0, (6, 0)$
   $x = 10, y = 2, (10, 2)$
   $x = 14, y = 4, (14, 4)$
   $x = 16, y = 5, (16, 5)$

page 42

1. (–6, 6)	7. (–3, –8)
2. (5, 4)	8. L
3. (3, –2)	9. J
4. (2, 5)	10. H
5. (–7, 3)	11. I
6. (–4, –4)	12. K

13–20. Check to see that student has drawn creatures at correct locations.

page 43

If student plots points and draws lines correctly, the result will be the drawing of a coiled snake.

pages 44–45

a. $x = -3, y = -2, (-3, -2)$
   $x = -2, y = 0, (-2, 0)$
   $x = -1, y = 2, (-1, 2)$
   $x = 0, y = 4, (0, 4)$

b. $x = -2, y = 2, (-2, 2)$
   $x = 1, y = -1, (1, -1)$
   $x = 2, y = -2, (2, -2)$
   $x = 3, y = -3, (3, -3)$
   $x = 4, y = -4, (4, -4)$

c. (–2, –4); (–1, –2); (0, 0);
   (1, 2); (2, 4)

d. (–1, 3); (0, 1); (1, –1); (2, –3)

e. (–4, 1); (–3, 2); (–2, 3); (–1, 4)

f. c

pages 46–47

1. (5, 3)
2. (5, –1)
3. (1, –3)
4. (1, 4)
5–7. These three answers may be in any order:
   (0, 5) corresponds to (3, 2)
   (–3, 2) corresponds to (0, –1)
   (–5, 4) corresponds to (–2, 1)
8. F
9. S
10. T
11. (1, 6) Check student grid to see that correct reflection of the figure has been drawn.
12–14. These three answers may be in any order.
   (–3, 6) corresponds to (3, 6)
   (–5, –2) corresponds to (5, –2)
   (–1, –2) corresponds to (1, –2)
   Check student grid to see that transformation of the hiker has been drawn with correct corresponding points.

pages 48–49

Check student drawings to see that sequences are correct.

page 50

Proportions may differ, depending on the order student chooses to write the terms. These are likely proportions. The solutions should not differ.

1. $4.5/2 = x/6$ .... Answer: 13.5 miles
2. $21/3 = 35/x$ .... Answer: 5 hours
3. $0.75/3 = x/13$ .... Answer: 3.25 qt
4. $15/5 = x/3$ .... Answer: 9 times
5. $9/6 = 6/x$ .... Answer: 4 hours
6. $n = 4$
7. $n = 18$